الحروف العربية

First published in Great Britain in 2020 by
Heart of Islam
1st Floor
28 Saxby Street
Leicester LE2 0NE

The Arabic Alphabet © Heart of Islam, 2020

Heart of Islam is an Imprint of AFFA House

Printed and bound in the E.U.

All rights reserved. Without limiting the rights under copyright reserved above, no part of this publication may be reproduced, stored or introduced into a retrieval system, or transmitted, in any form or by any means (electronic, mechanical, photocopying, recording or otherwise), without the prior written permission of the publisher of this book.

ISBN 978-1-9998719-3-2

الحروف العربية

Designed by Azhar Majothi

heartofislam

2020

Knowledge is only obtained through learning.

Hadith

Designer's Note

This book is designed for students of all ages who wish to begin learning the beautiful language of Arabic.

The first stage for anyone wishing to do so is to learn the alphabet. And so you will find in the following spreads, each of the 28 letters of the alphabet along with visual examples of how the letter is written, how the letter appears in the beginning, middle and end of a word and a corresponding noun. It is easy to follow alone but it is highly recommended that you learn the letters with a teacher, particularly the pronunciation.

I hope that this book helps you on your journey; thank you for your support.

Azhar Majothi

The Arabic Alphabet

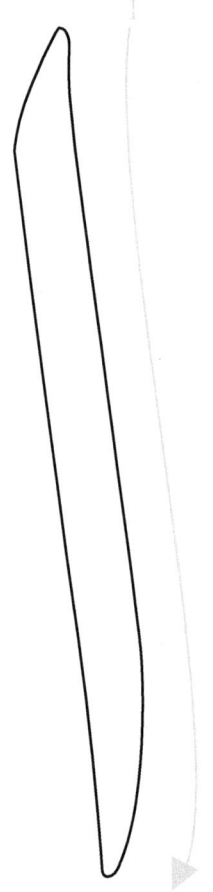

The Arabic Alphabet

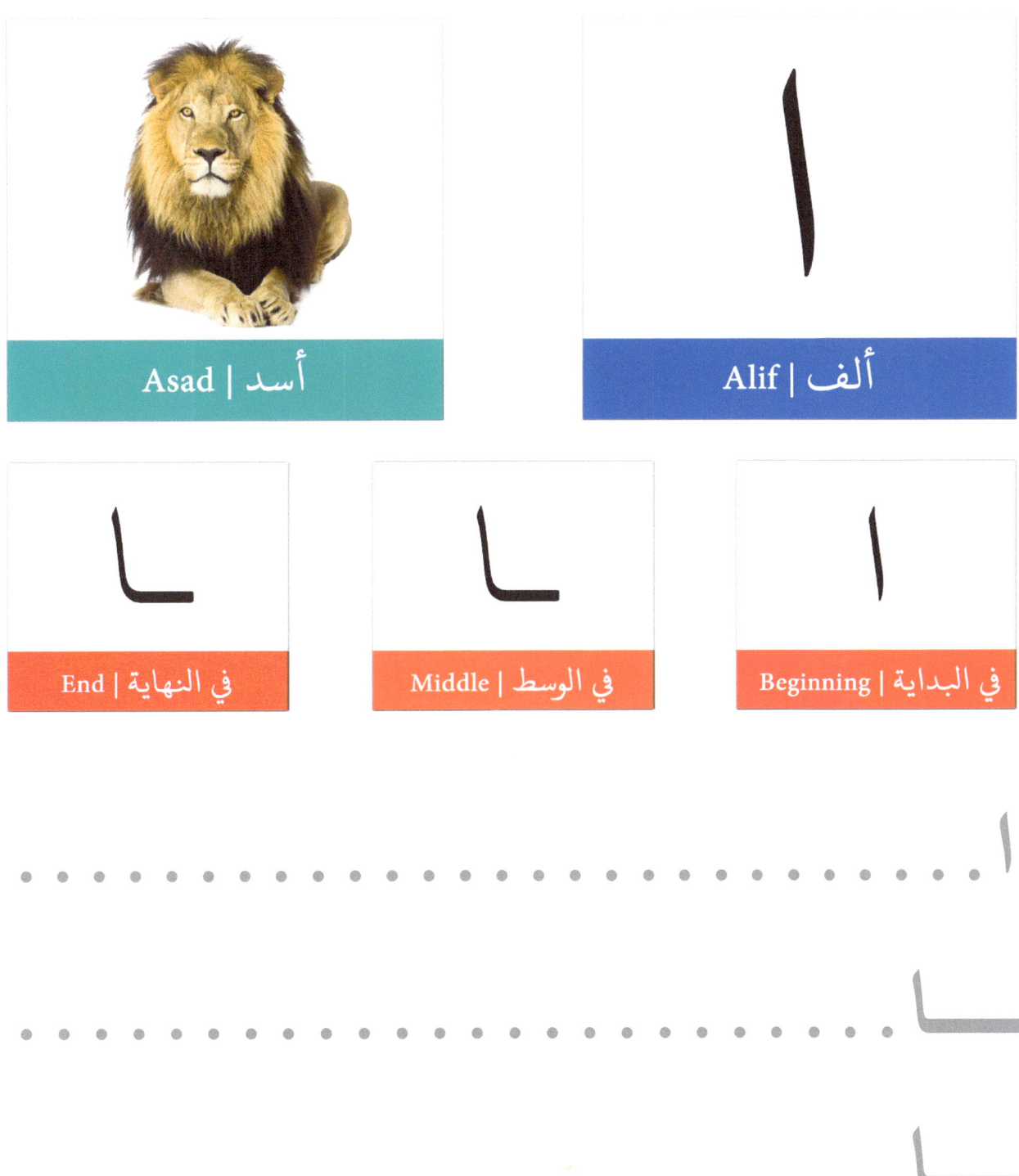

The Arabic Alphabet

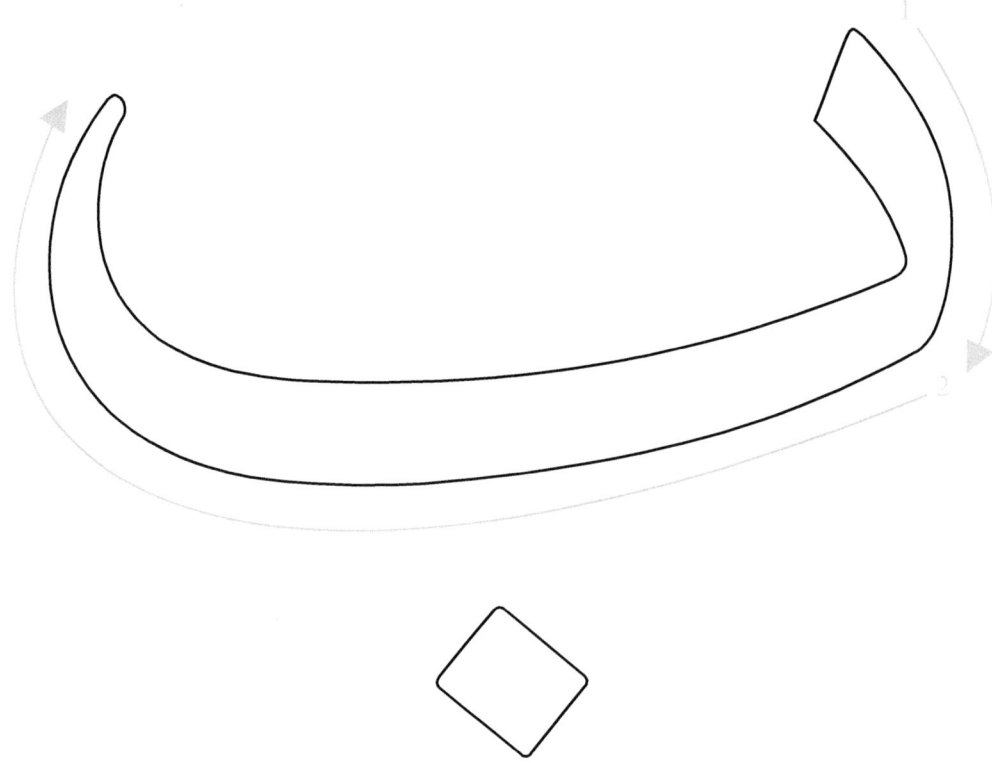

The Arabic Alphabet

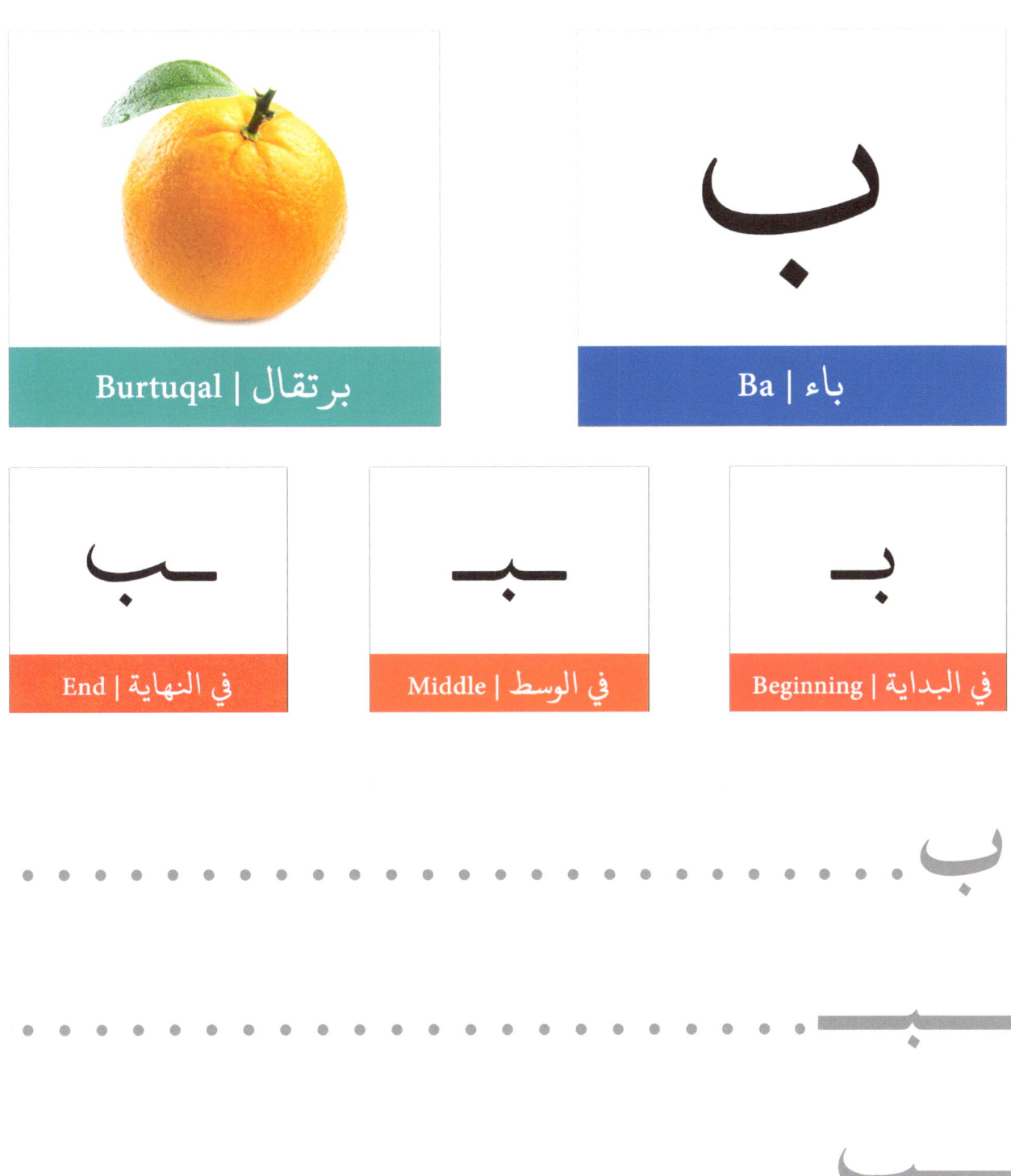

ب

The Arabic Alphabet

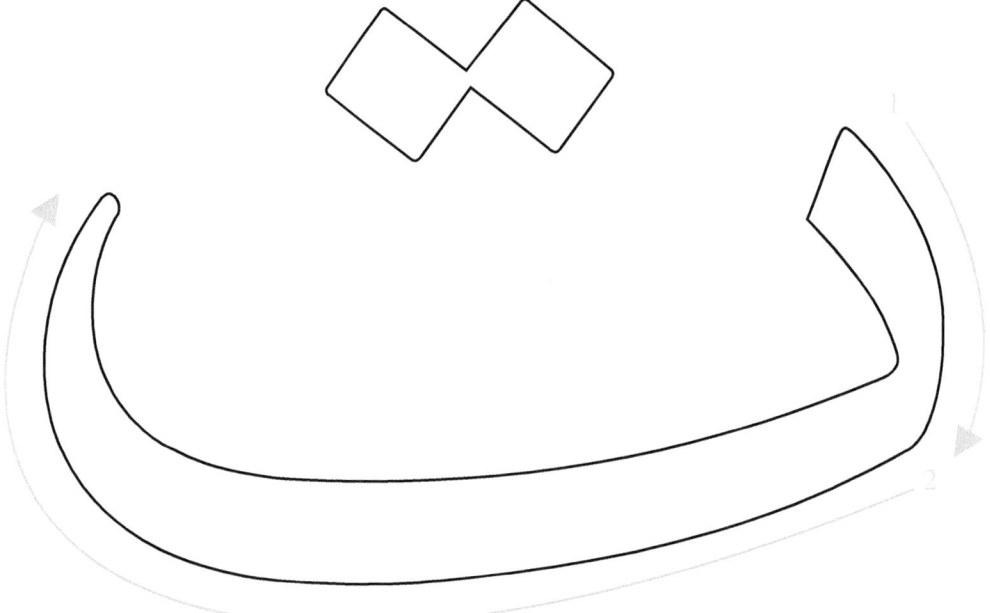

The Arabic Alphabet

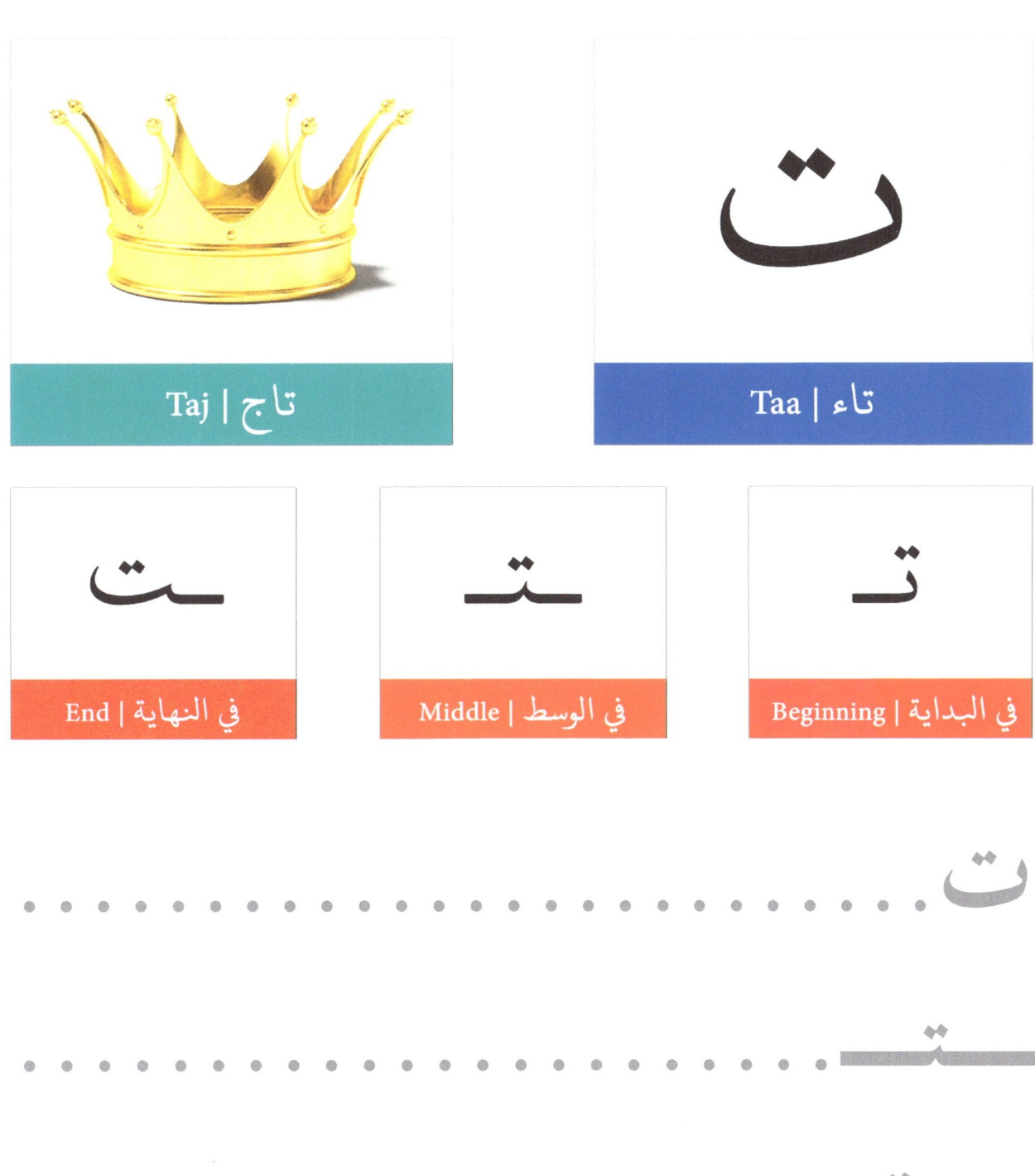

11

The Arabic Alphabet

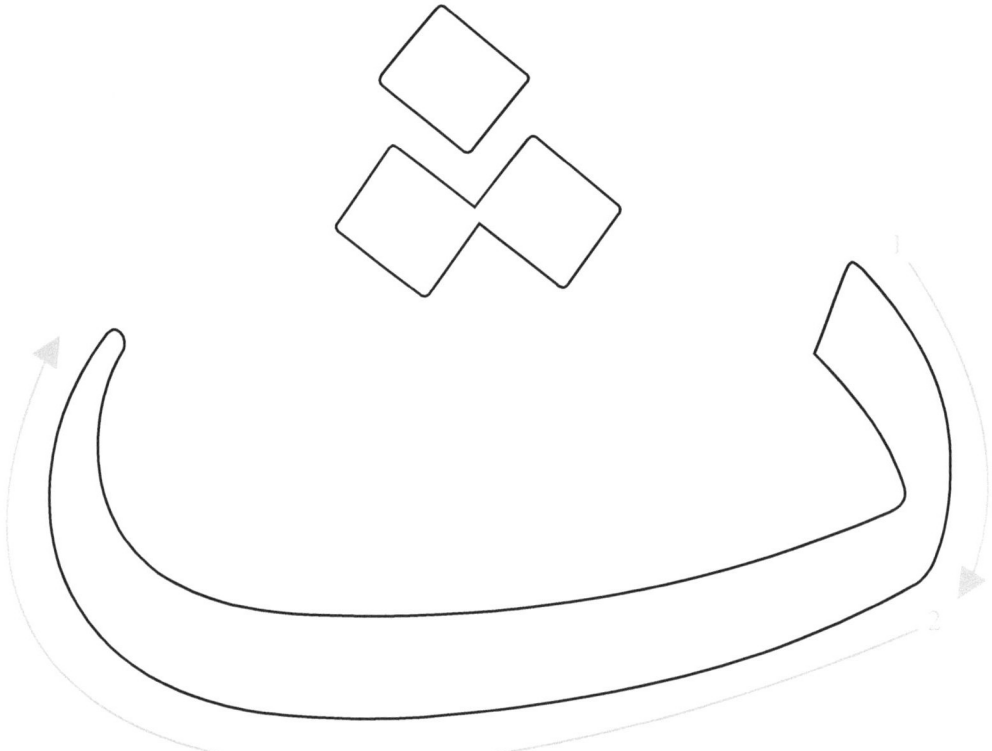

The Arabic Alphabet

13

The Arabic Alphabet

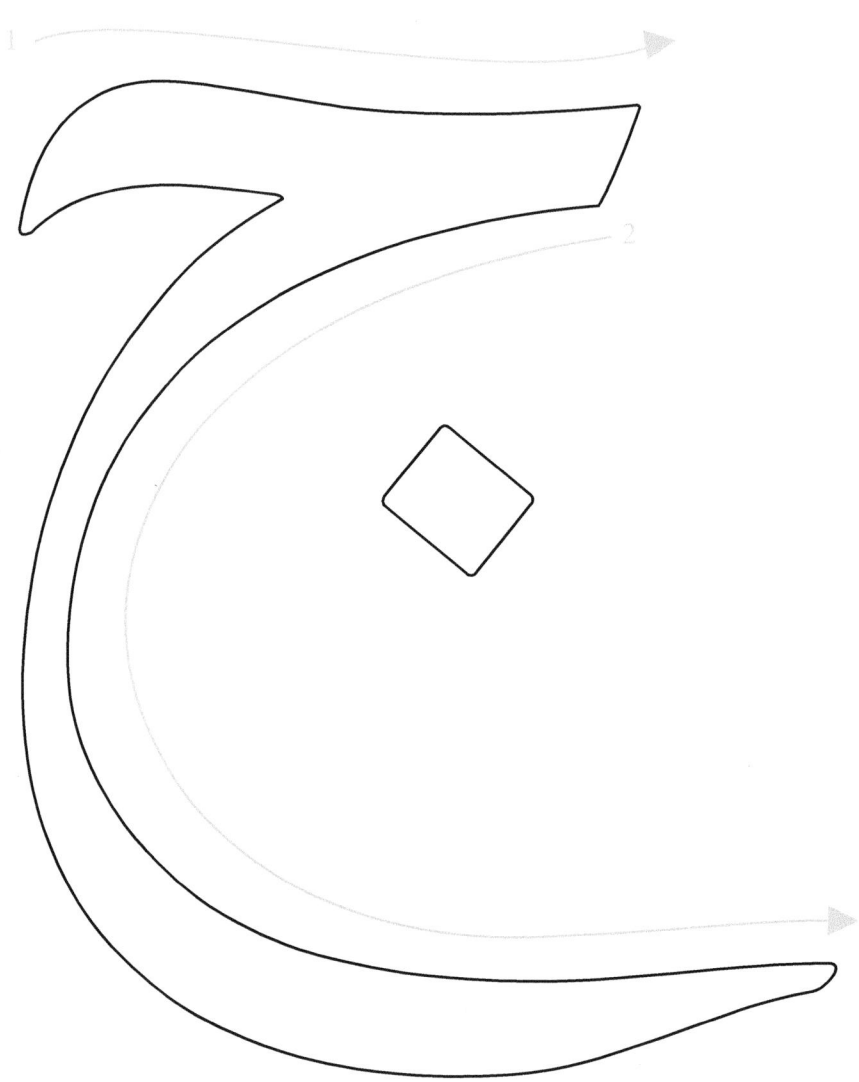

The Arabic Alphabet

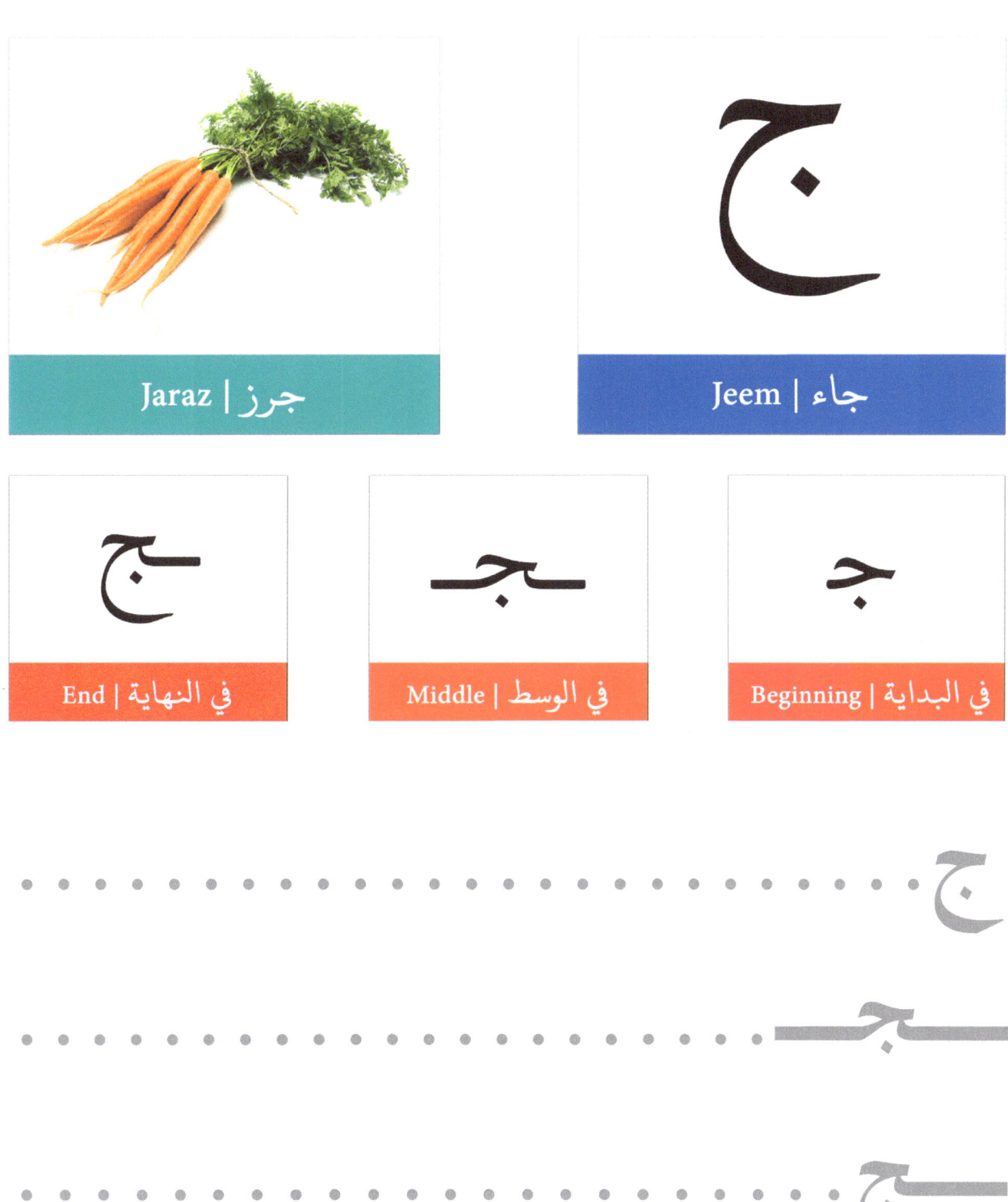

15

The Arabic Alphabet

The Arabic Alphabet

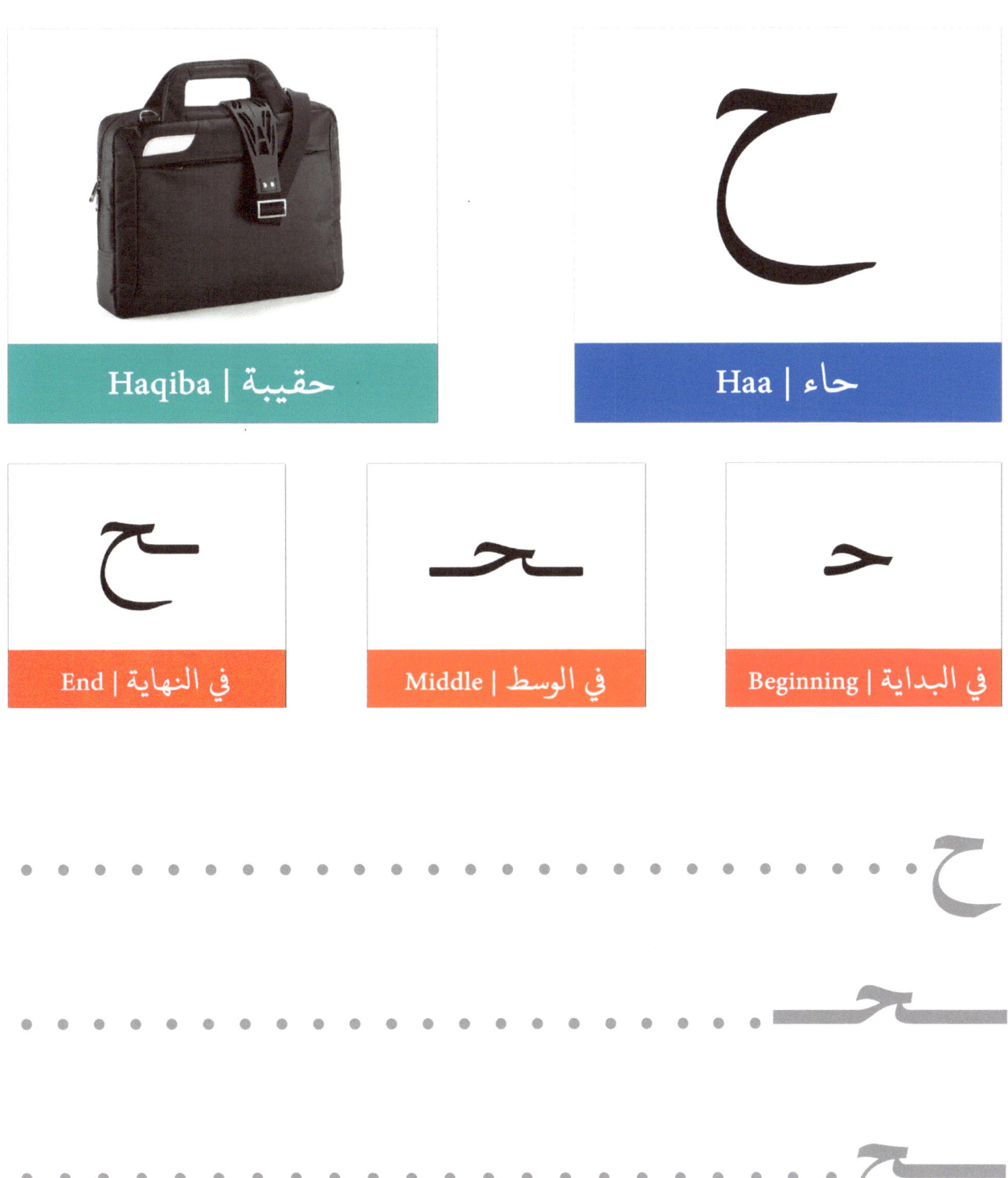

17

The Arabic Alphabet

The Arabic Alphabet

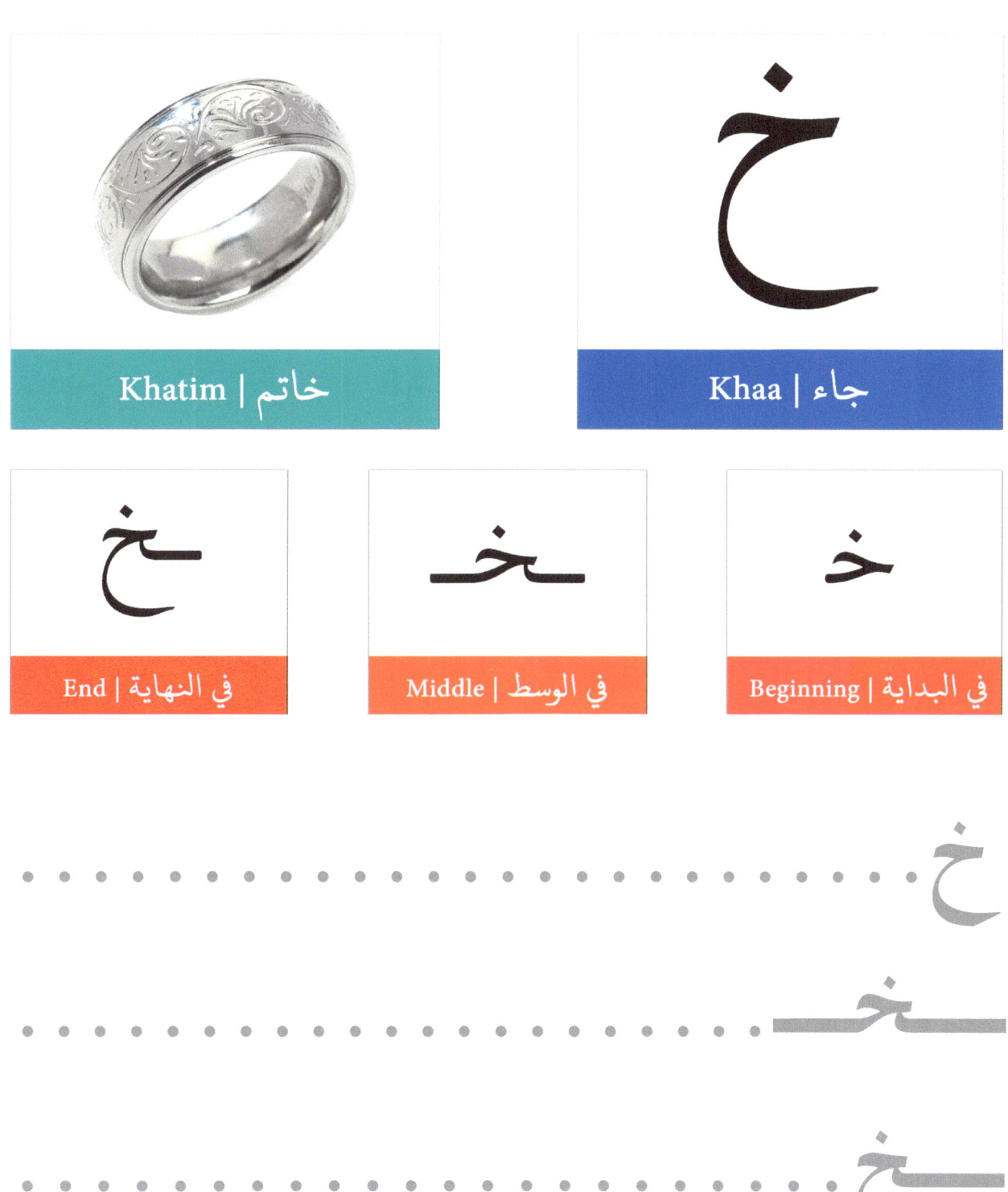

The Arabic Alphabet

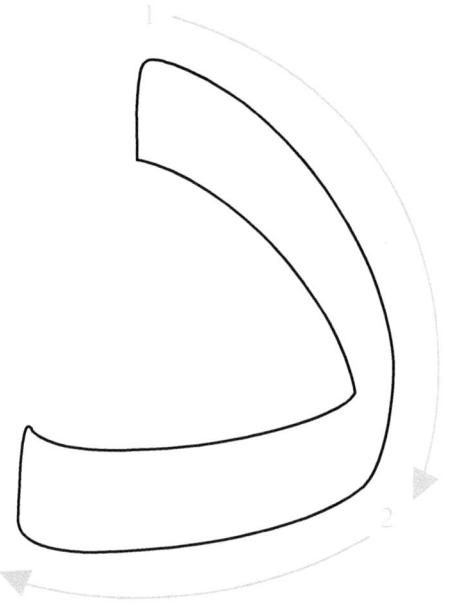

The Arabic Alphabet

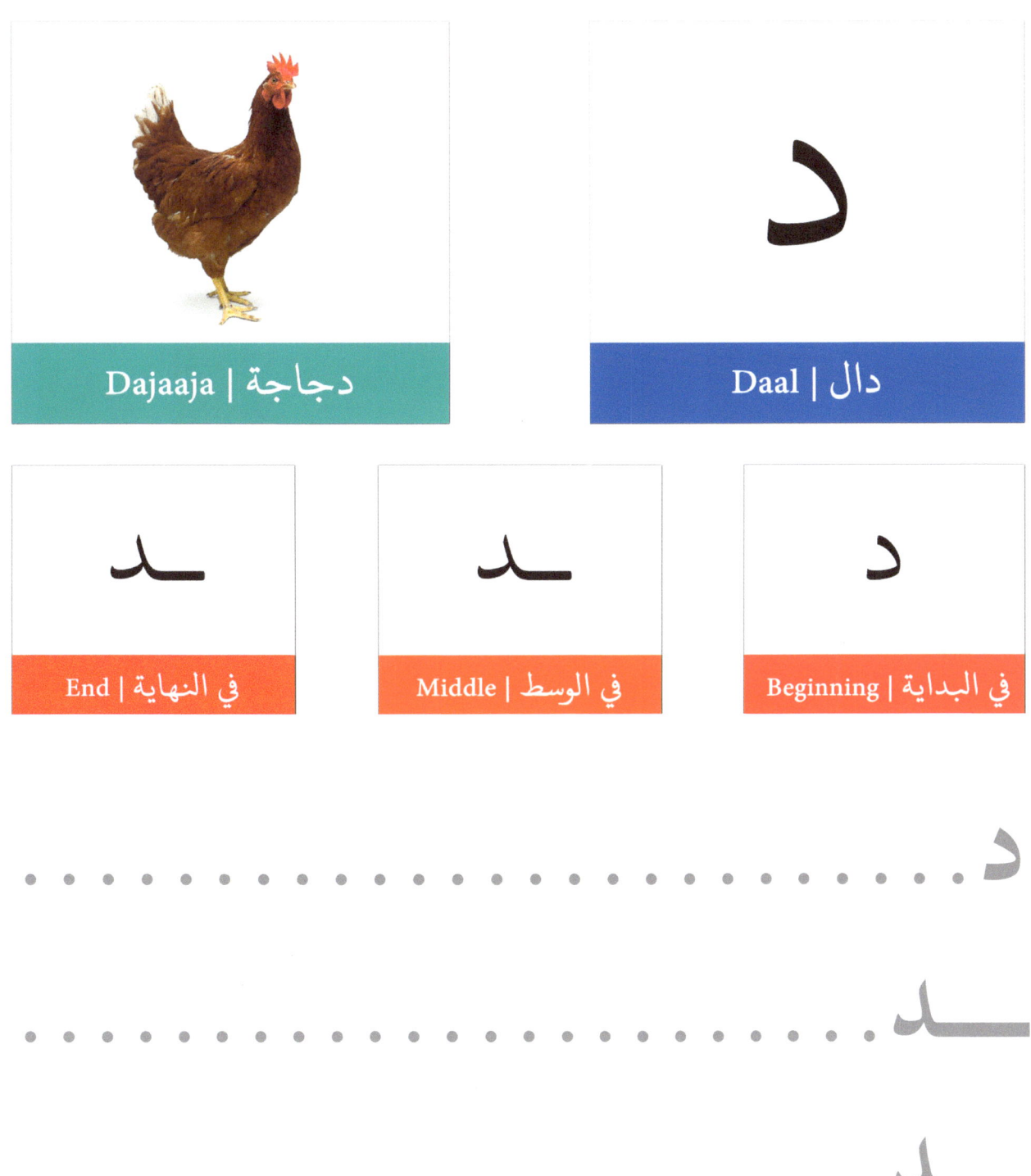

د ... د
ـد ... ـد
ـد ... ـد

The Arabic Alphabet

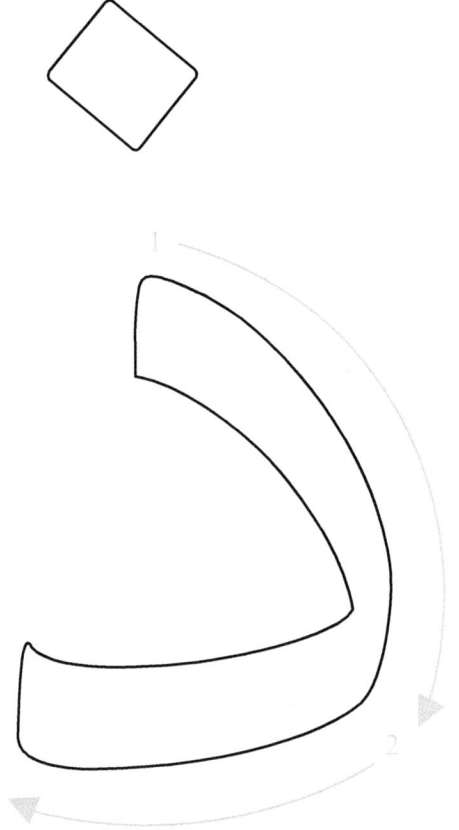

The Arabic Alphabet

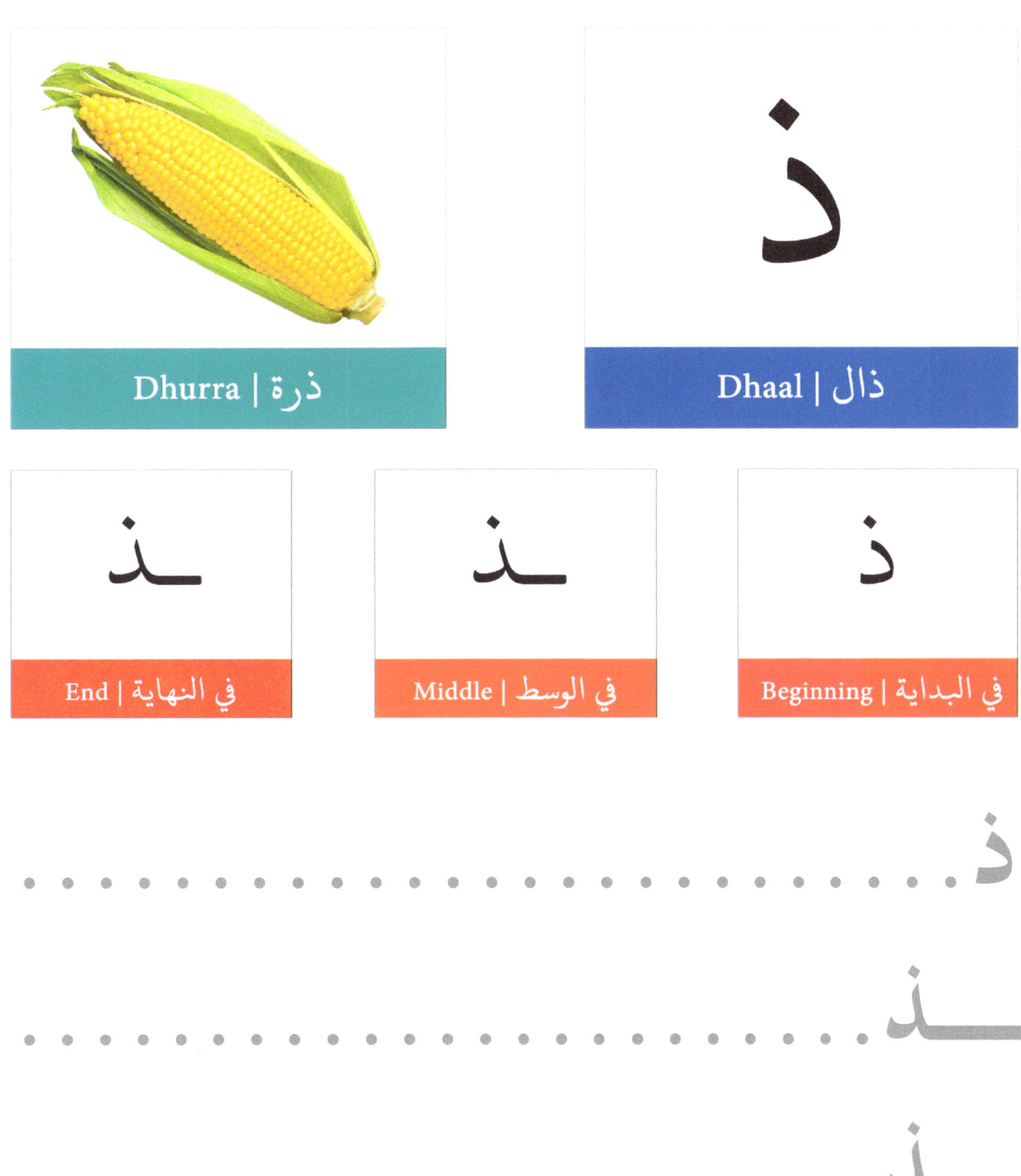

23

The Arabic Alphabet

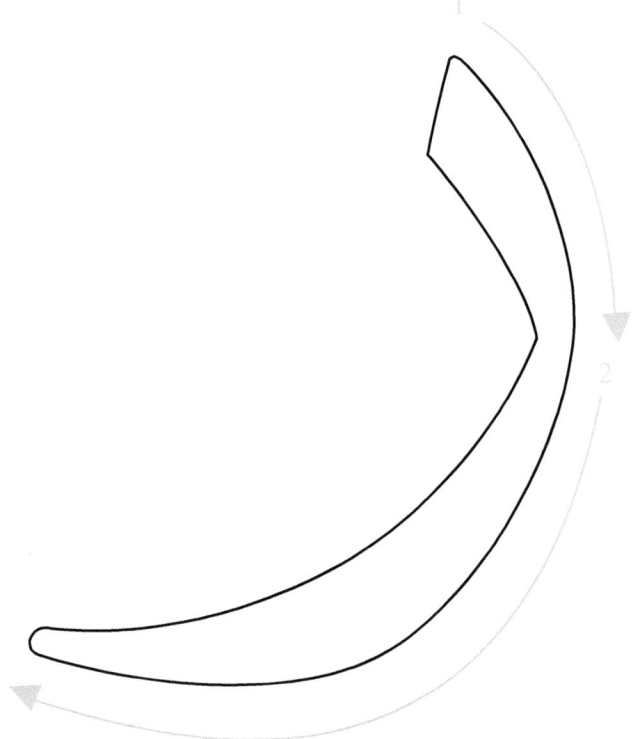

The Arabic Alphabet

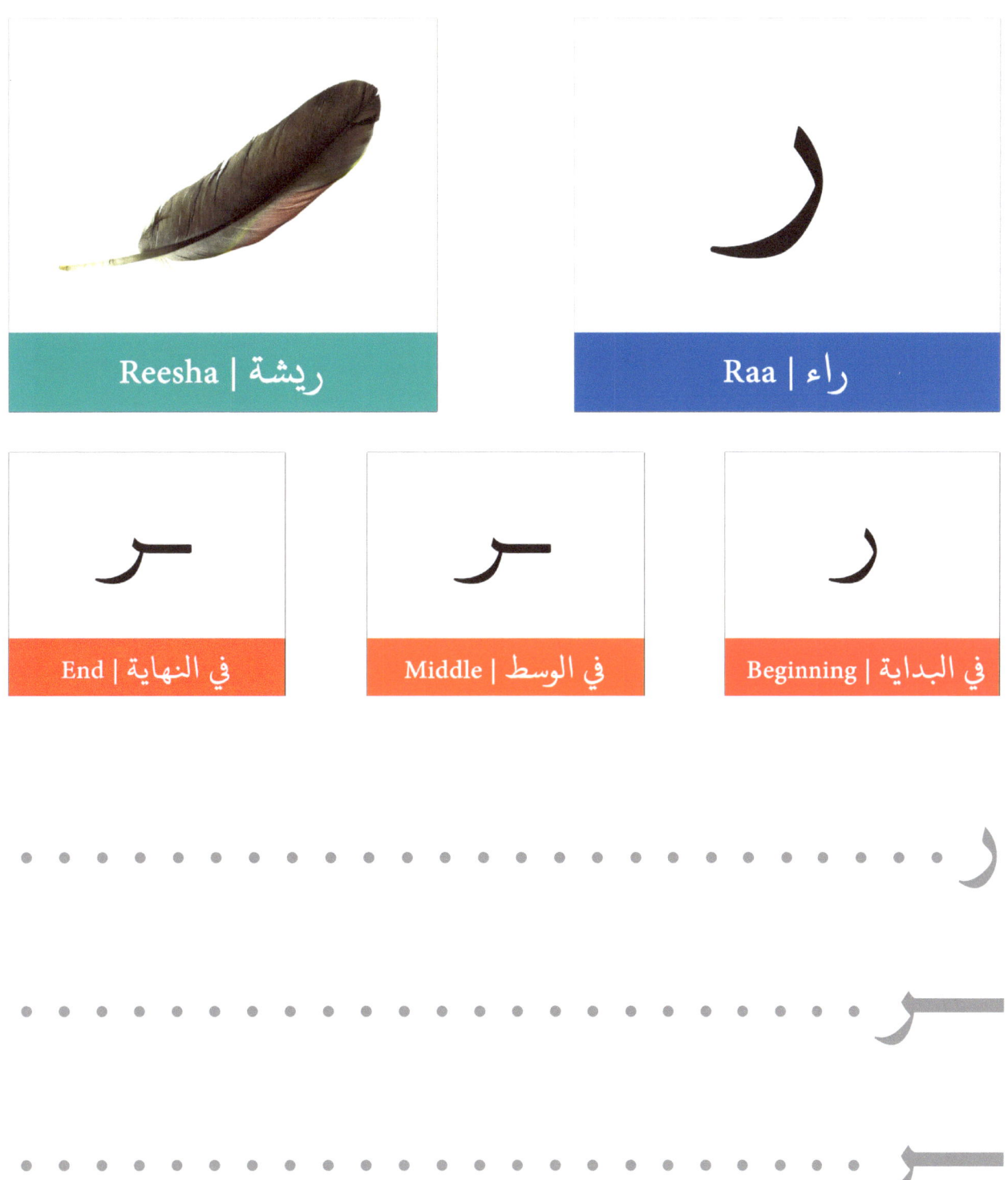

25

The Arabic Alphabet

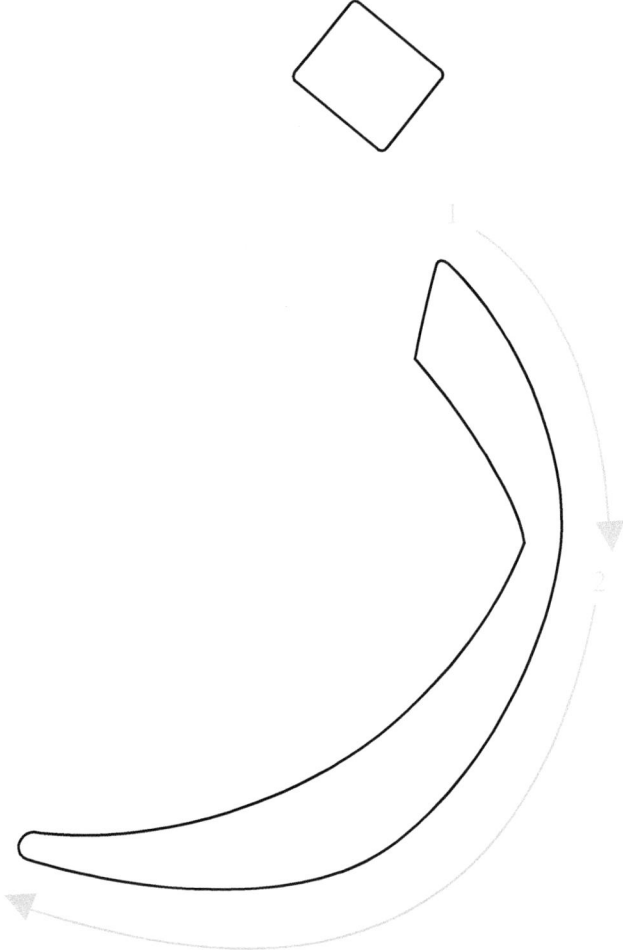

The Arabic Alphabet

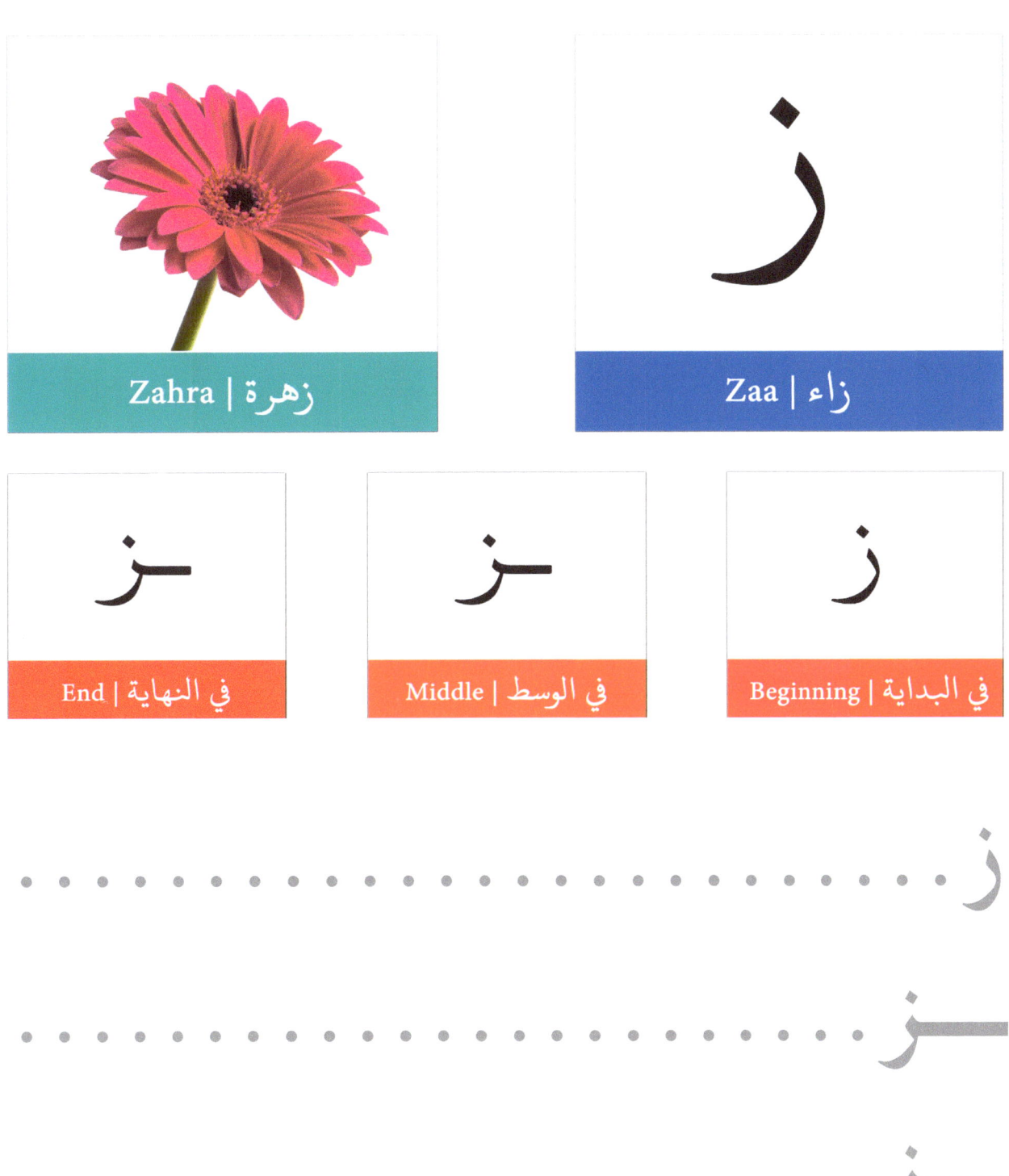

The Arabic Alphabet

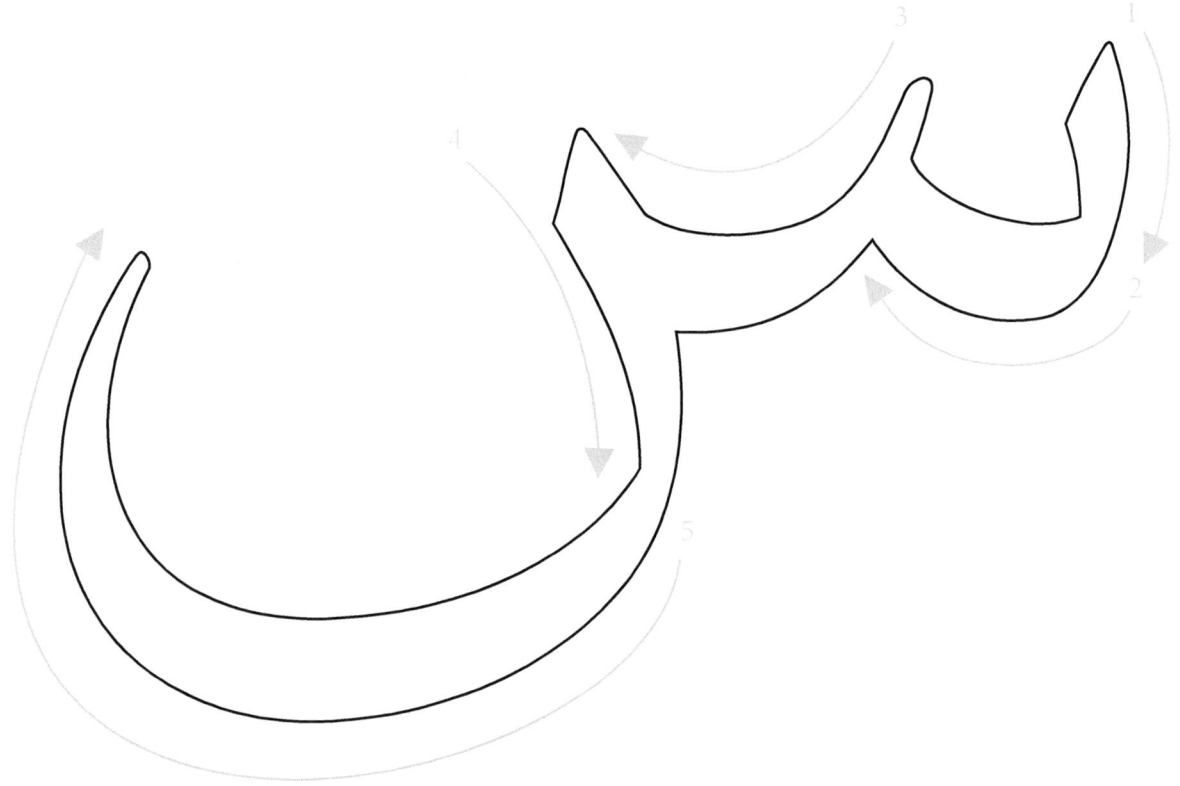

The Arabic Alphabet

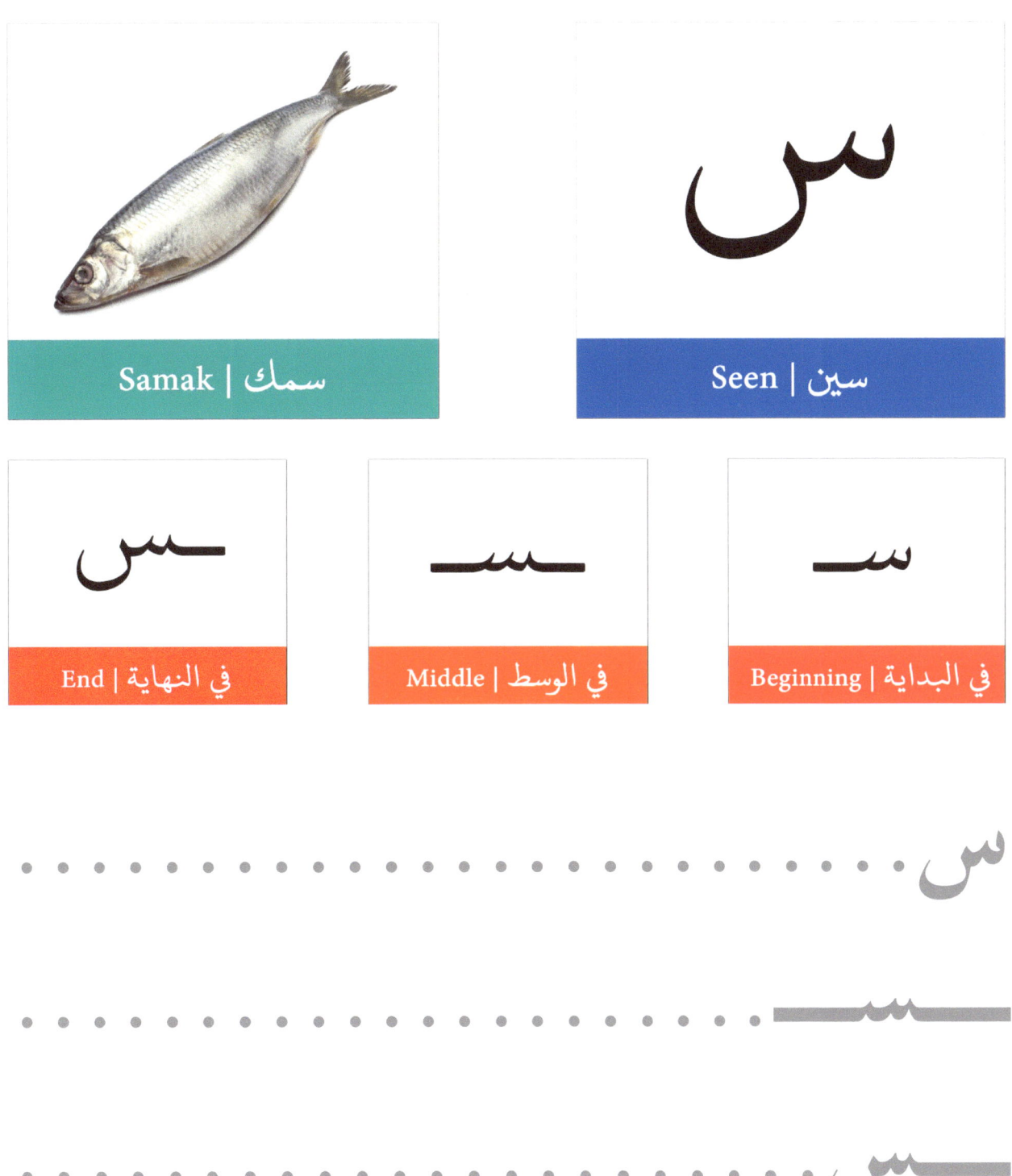

سمك | Samak

سين | Seen

في النهاية | End

في الوسط | Middle

في البداية | Beginning

29

The Arabic Alphabet

The Arabic Alphabet

شين | Sheen

شاحنة | Shaahina

في البداية | Beginning

في الوسط | Middle

في النهاية | End

The Arabic Alphabet

The Arabic Alphabet

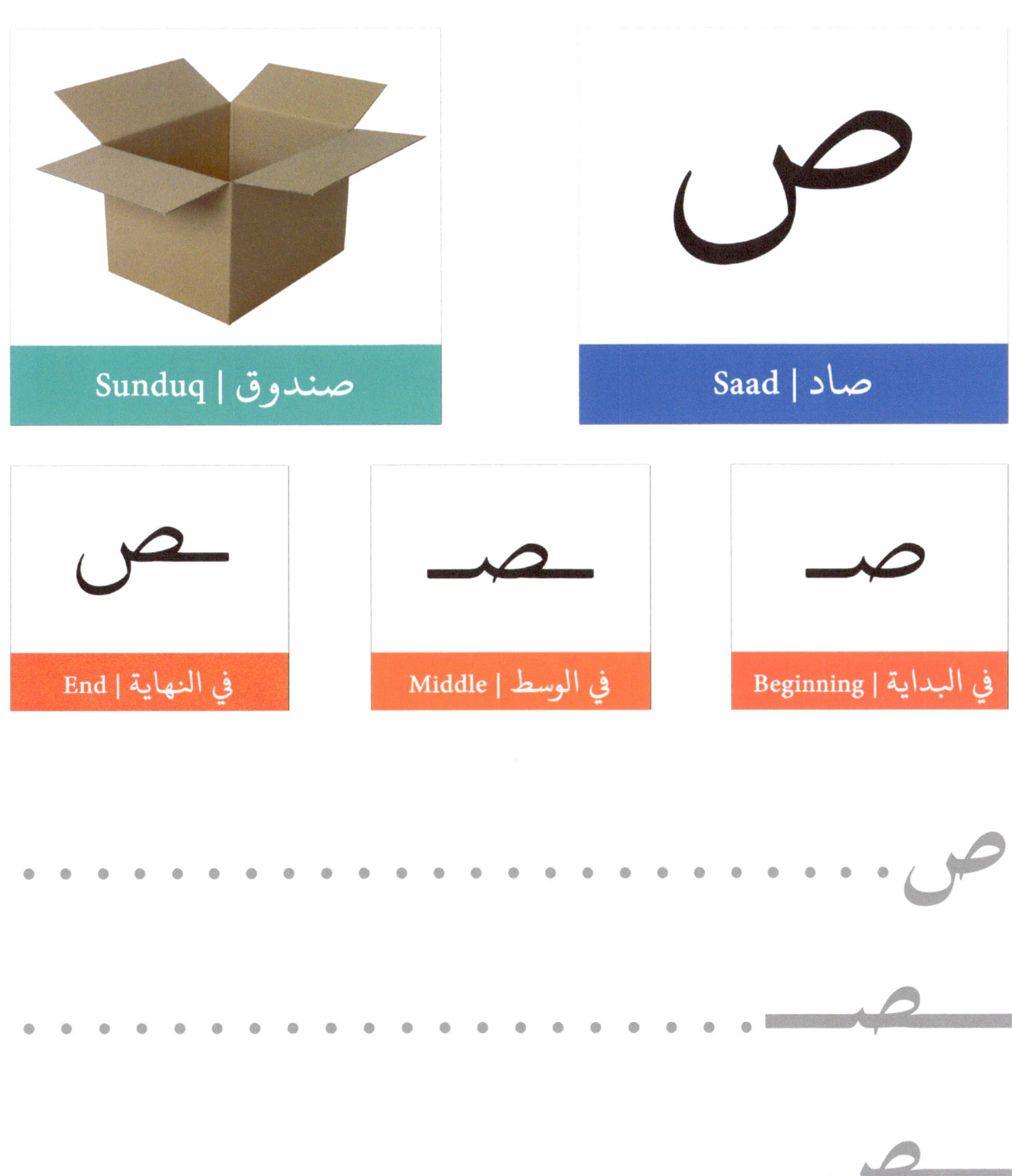

The Arabic Alphabet

The Arabic Alphabet

35

The Arabic Alphabet

The Arabic Alphabet

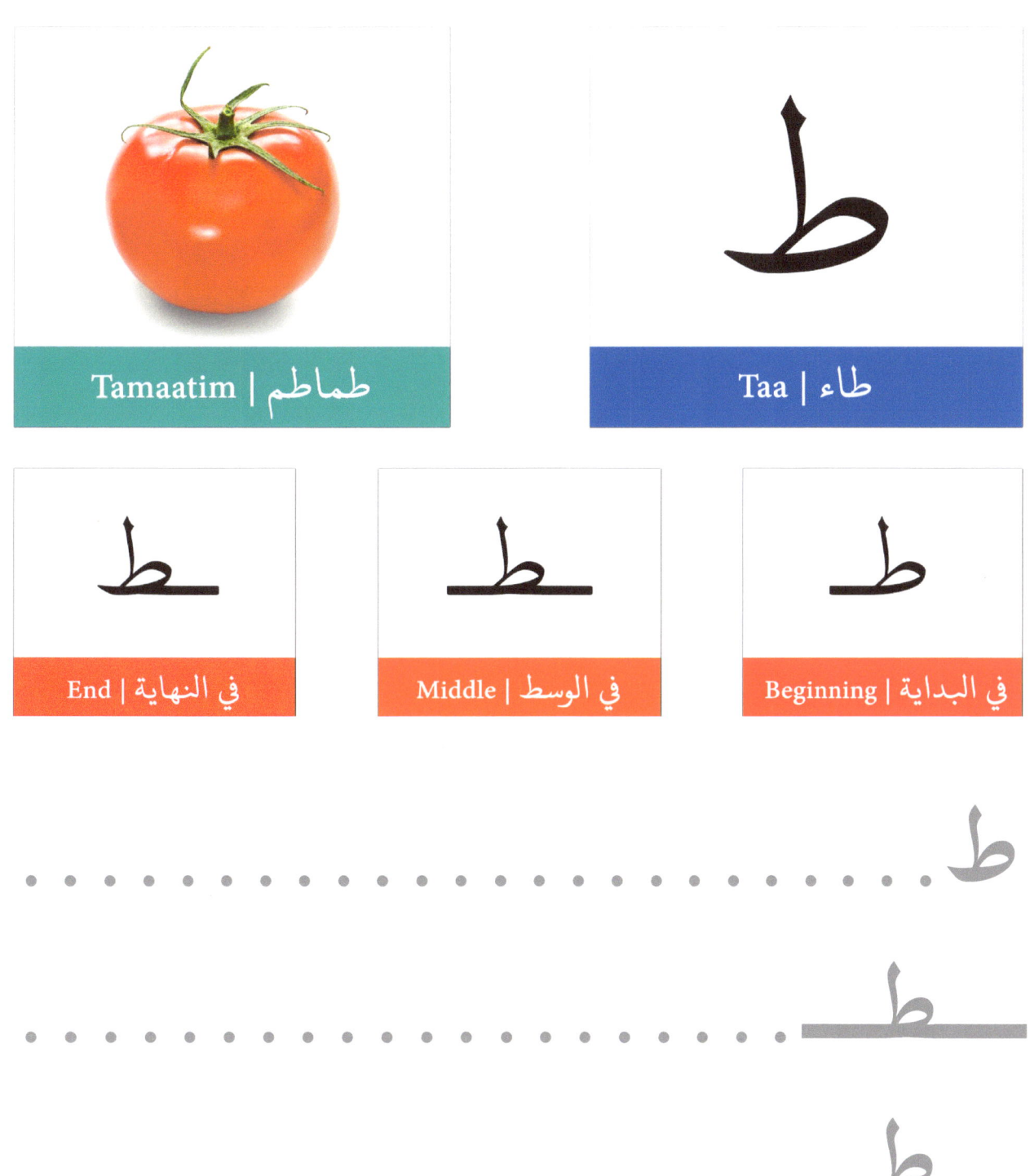

The Arabic Alphabet

The Arabic Alphabet

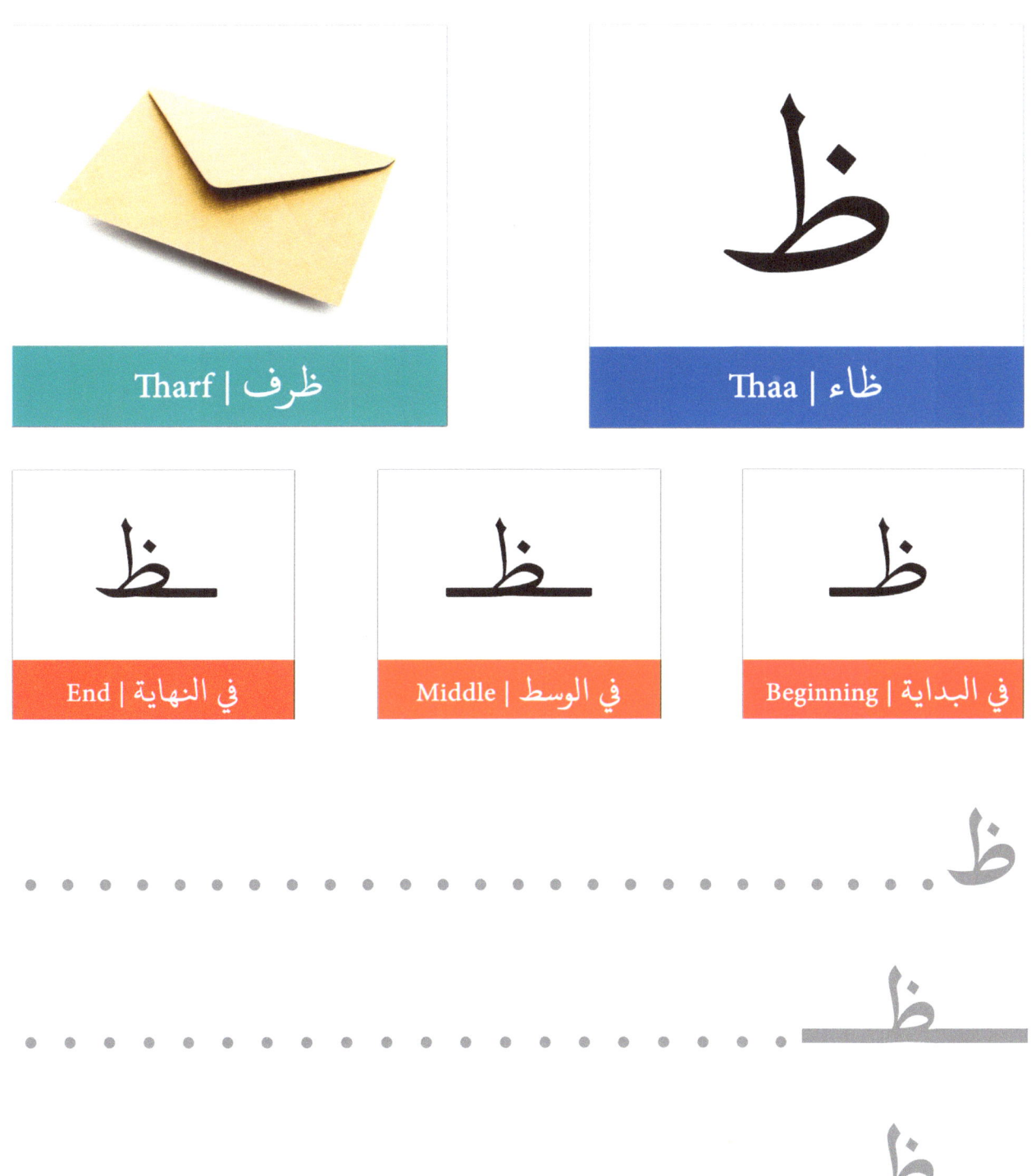

The Arabic Alphabet

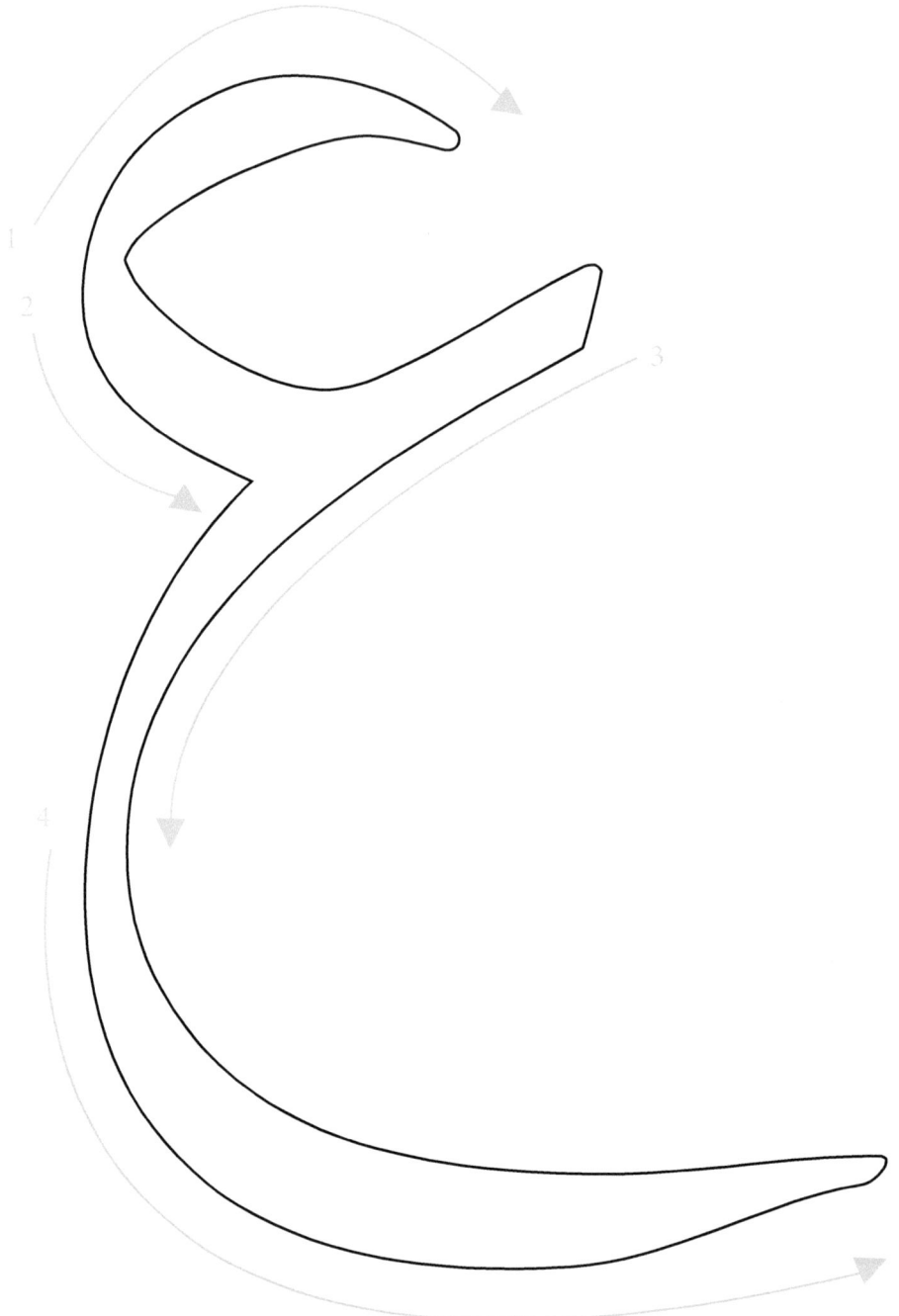

The Arabic Alphabet

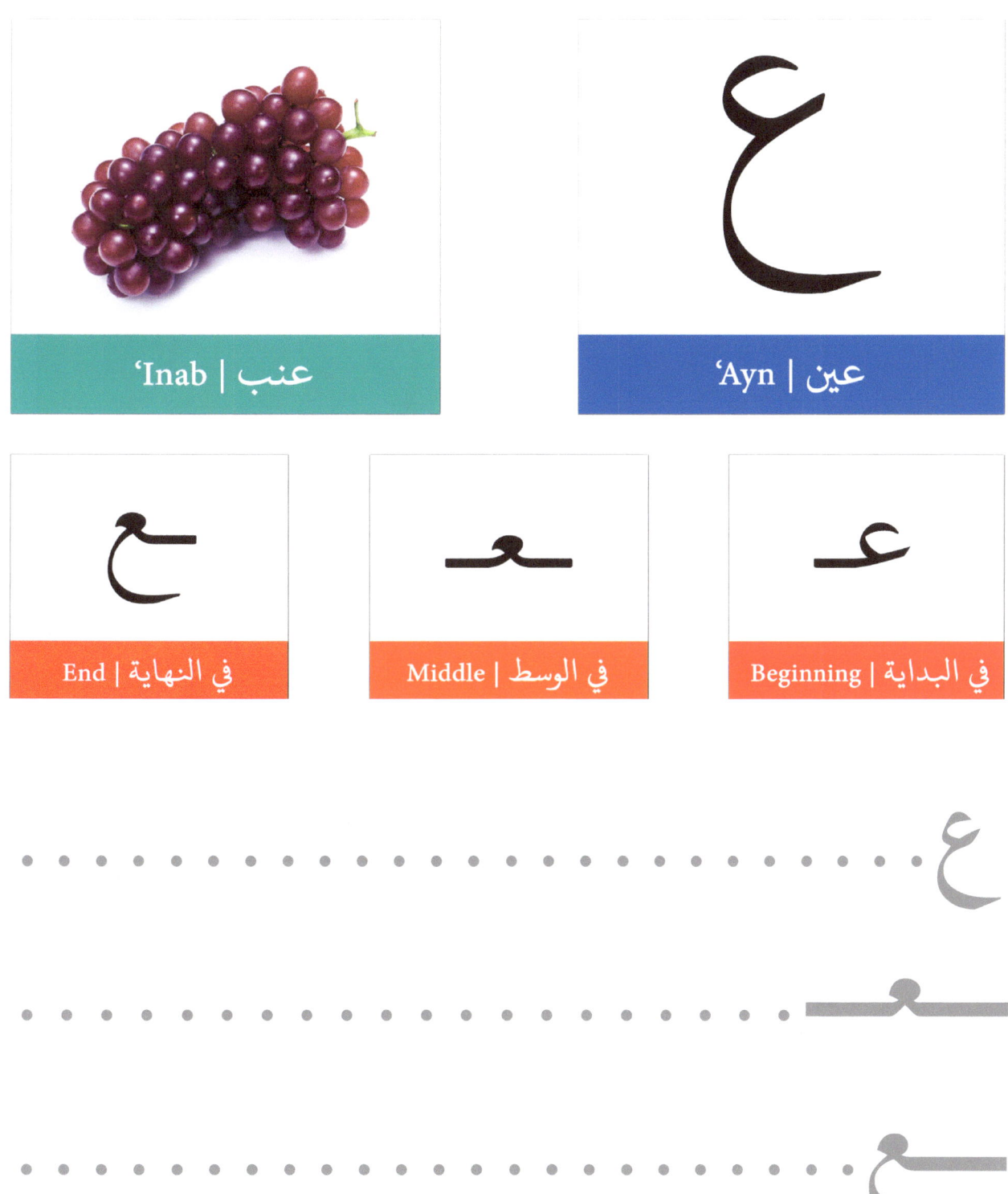

41

The Arabic Alphabet

The Arabic Alphabet

Gassala | غسالة

Ghayn | غين

End | في النهاية

Middle | في الوسط

Beginning | في البداية

The Arabic Alphabet

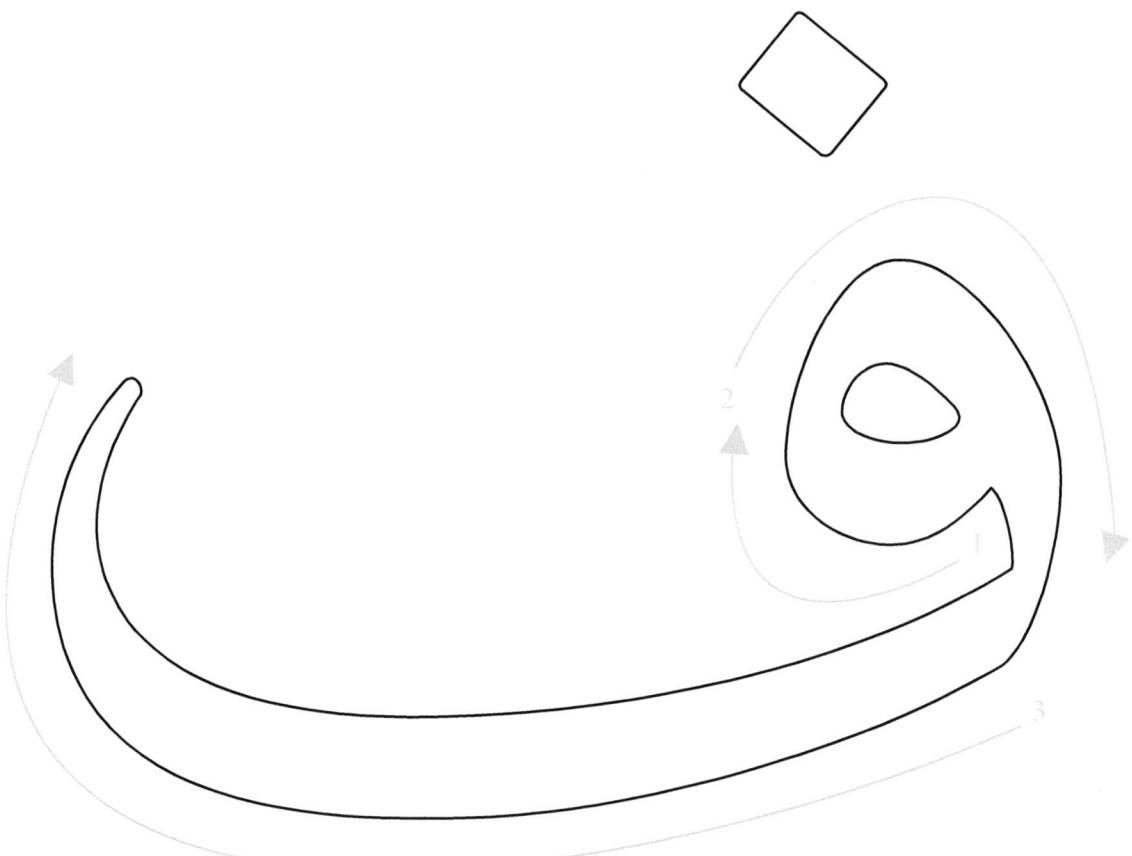

The Arabic Alphabet

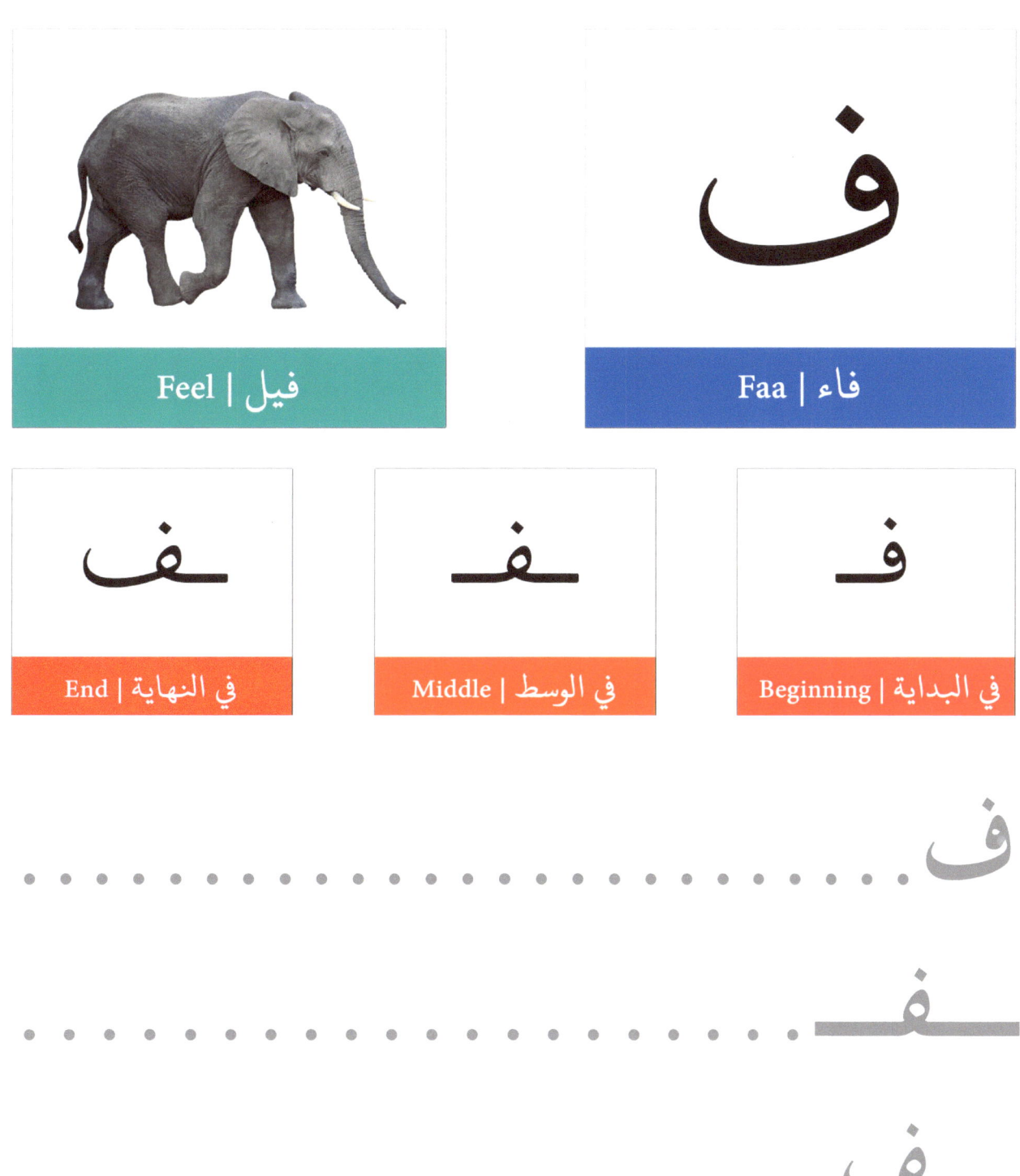

45

The Arabic Alphabet

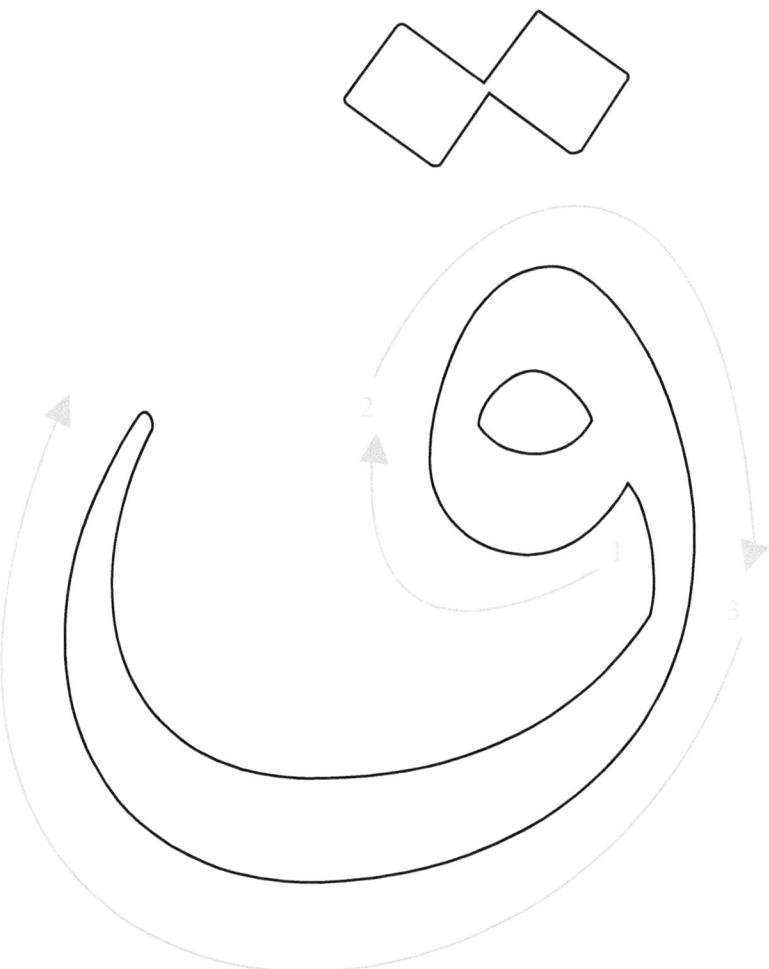

The Arabic Alphabet

The Arabic Alphabet

48

The Arabic Alphabet

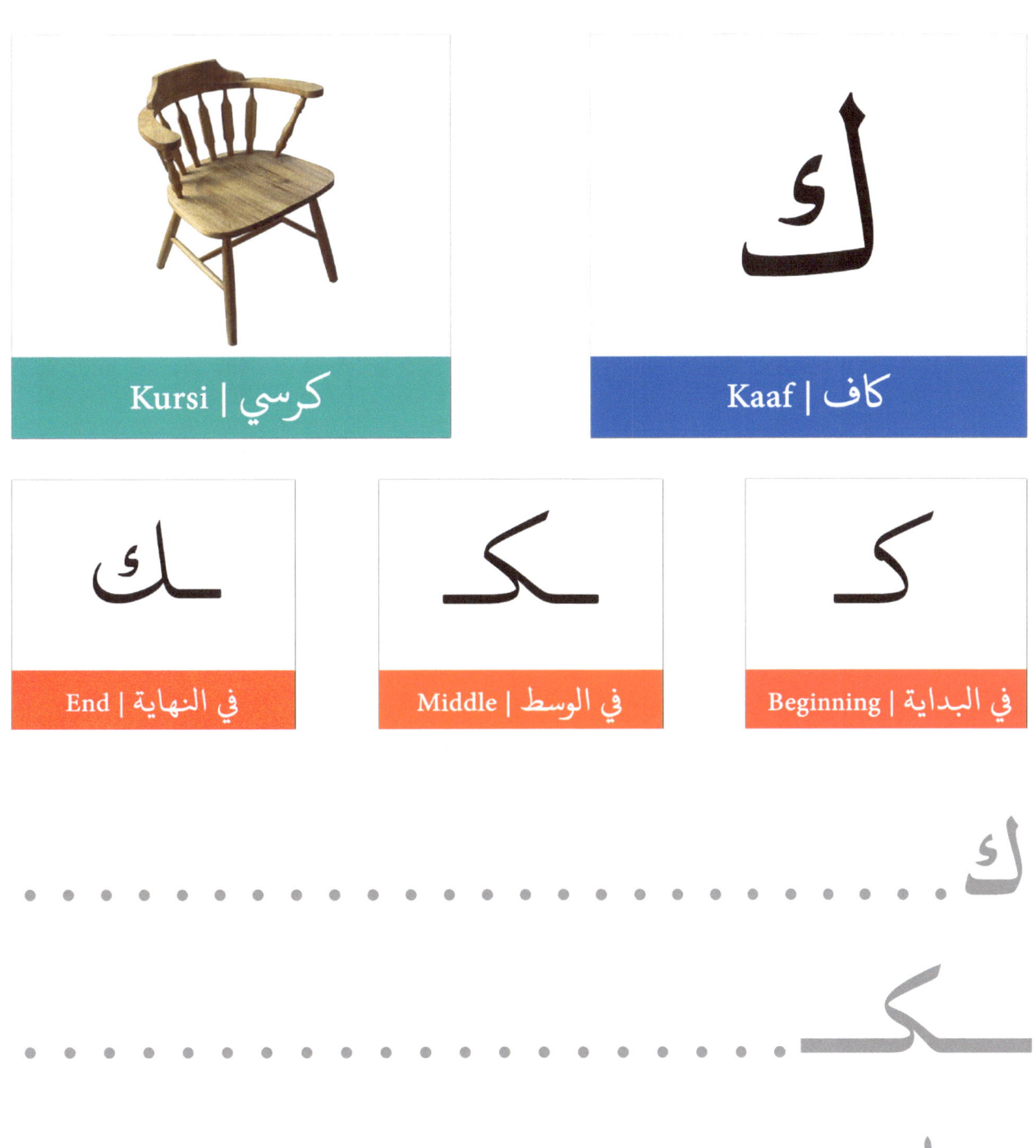

The Arabic Alphabet

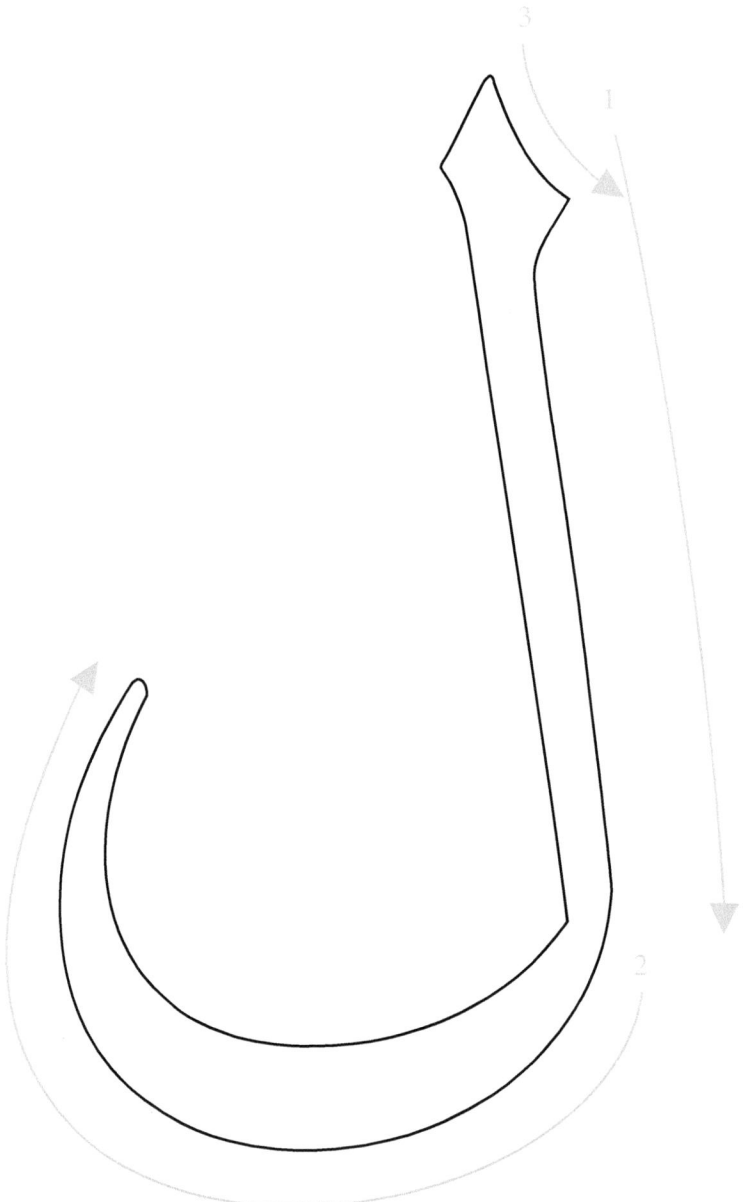

The Arabic Alphabet

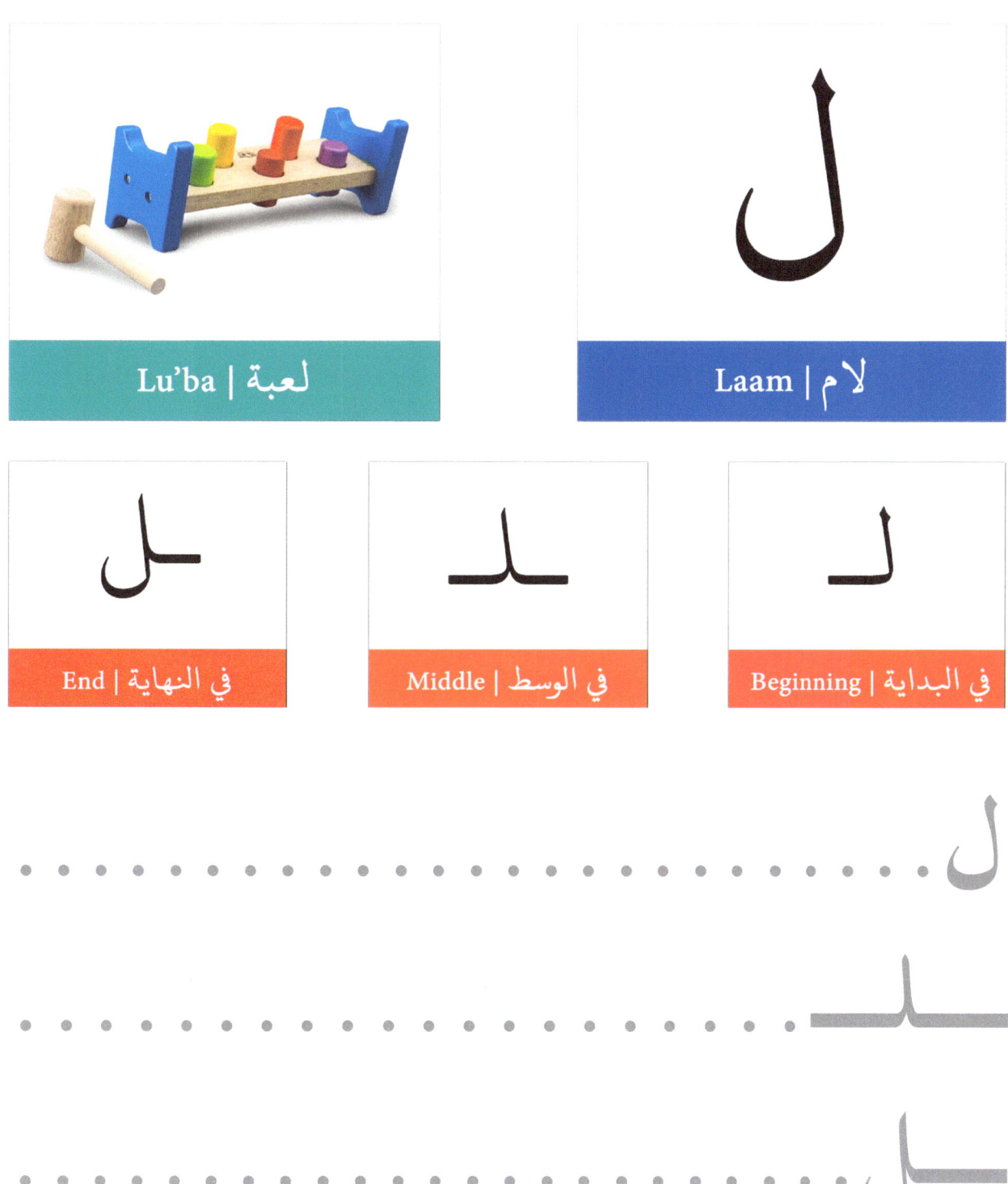

| لعبة \| Lu'ba | لام \| Laam |

| في النهاية \| End | في الوسط \| Middle | في البداية \| Beginning |

ل

ـلـ

ـل

51

The Arabic Alphabet

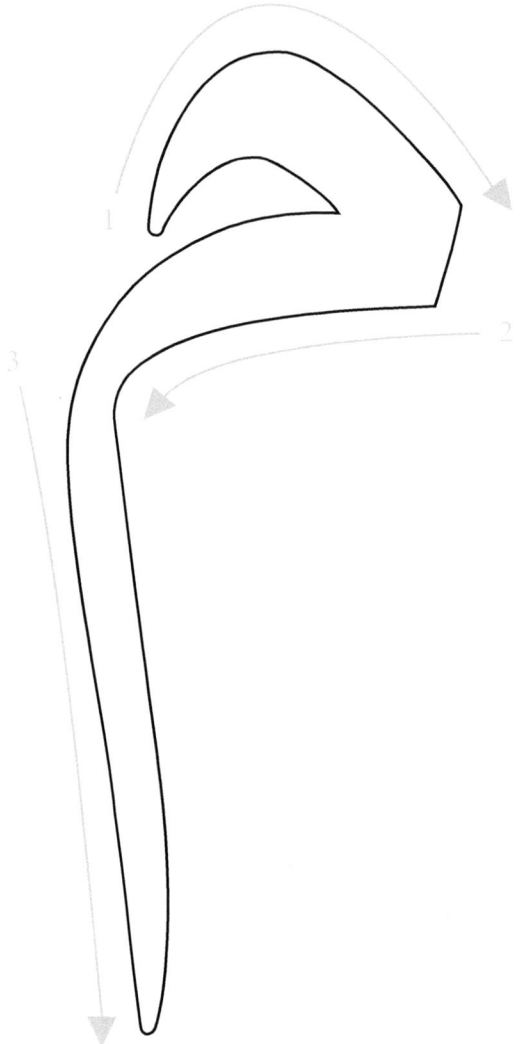

The Arabic Alphabet

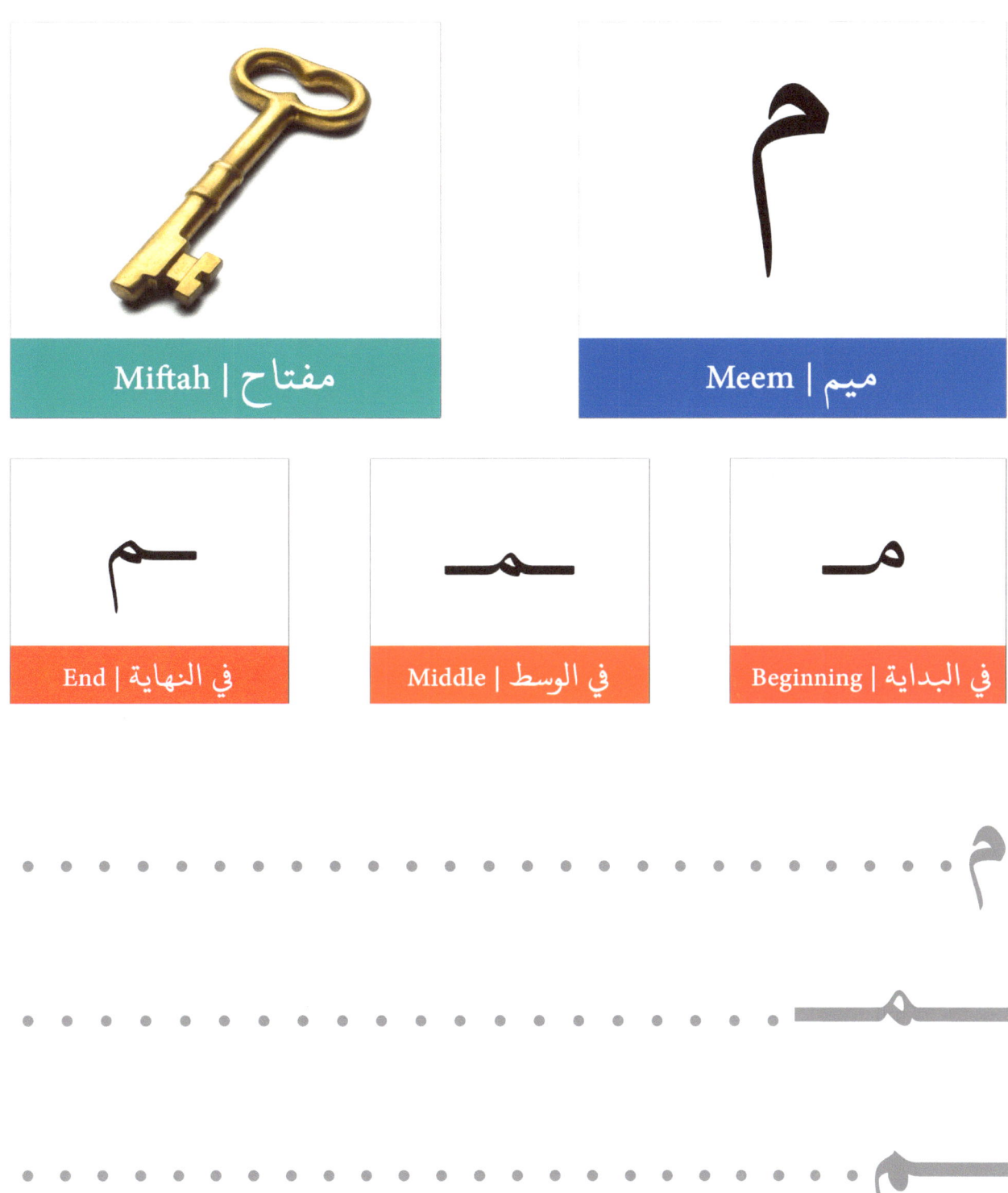

53

The Arabic Alphabet

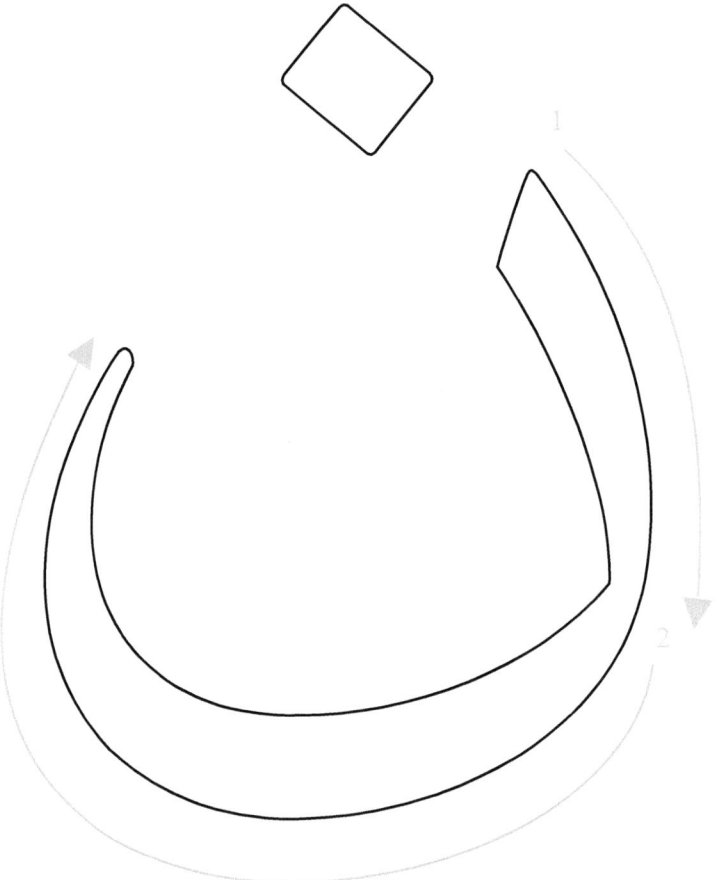

The Arabic Alphabet

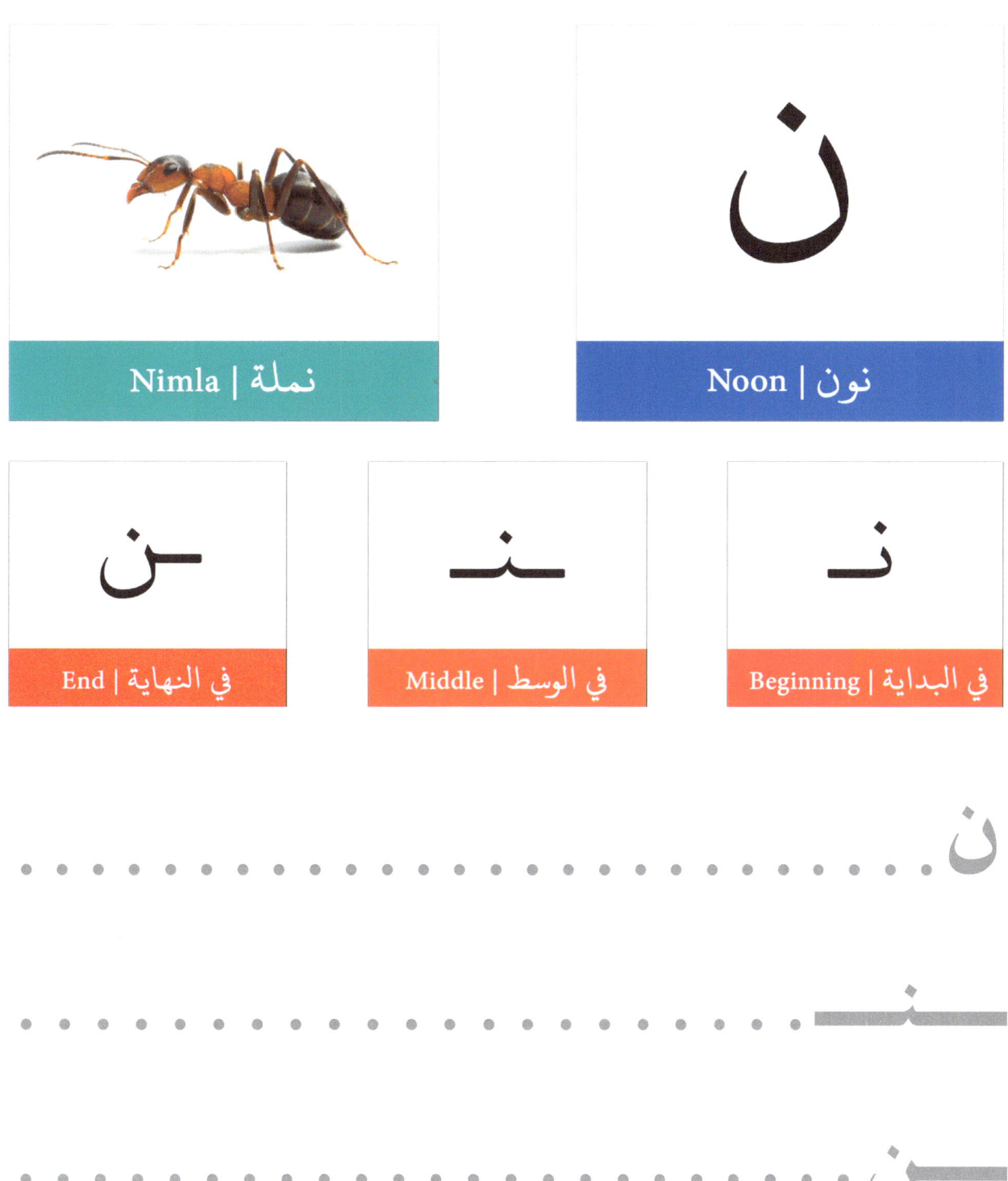

The Arabic Alphabet

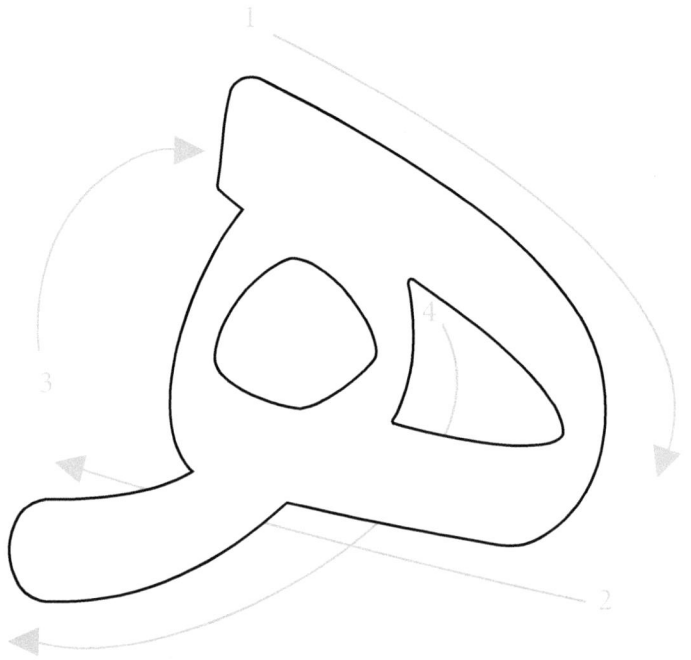

The Arabic Alphabet

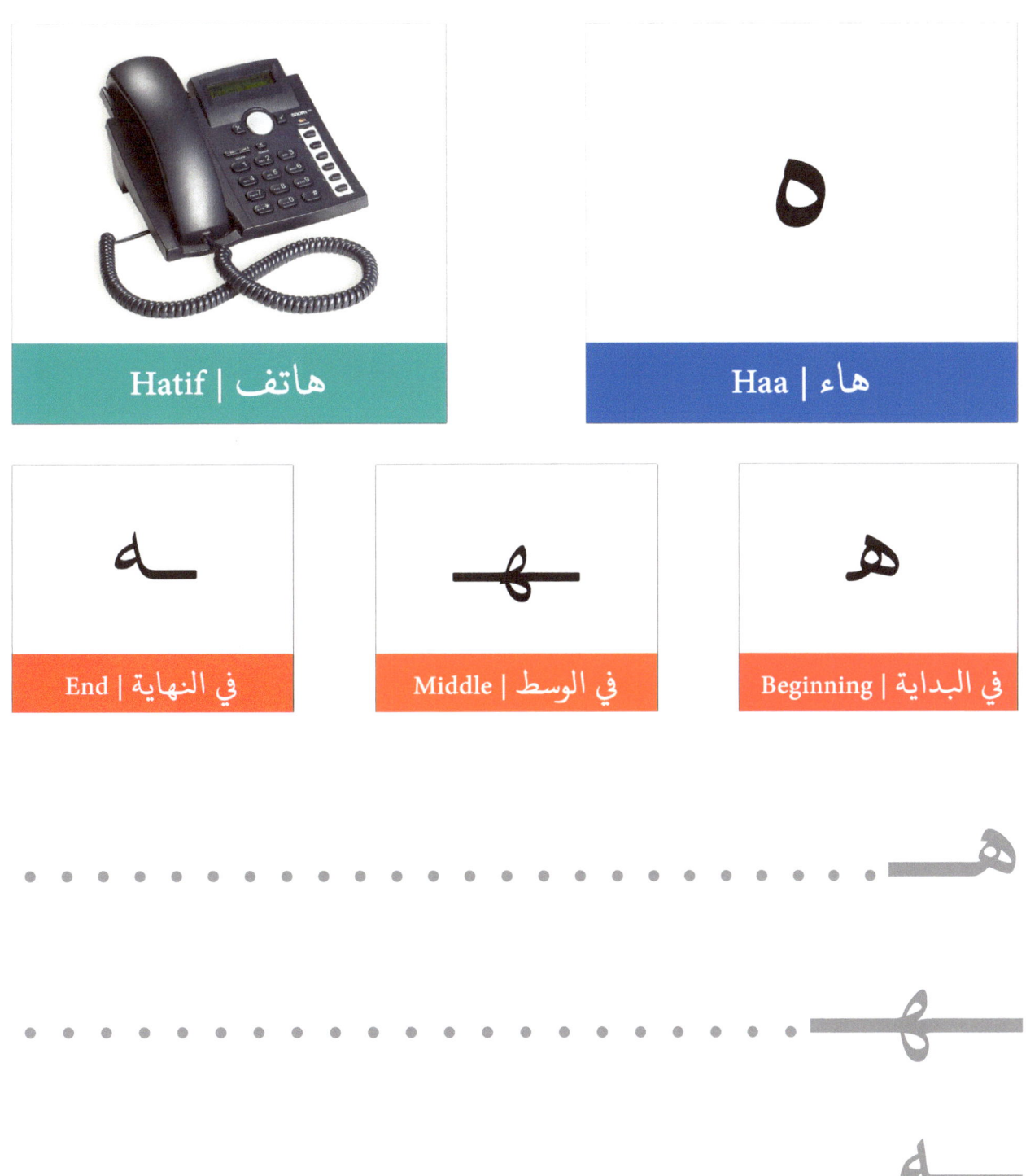

The Arabic Alphabet

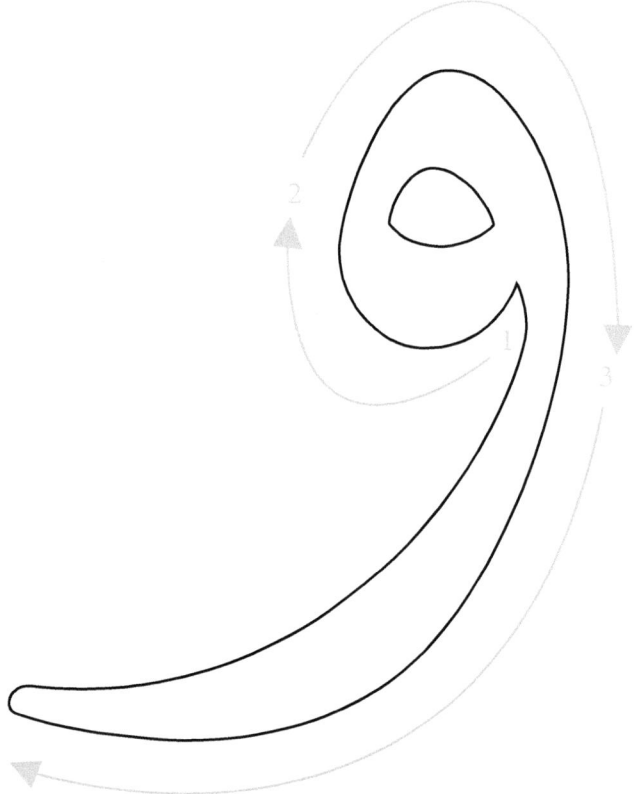

The Arabic Alphabet

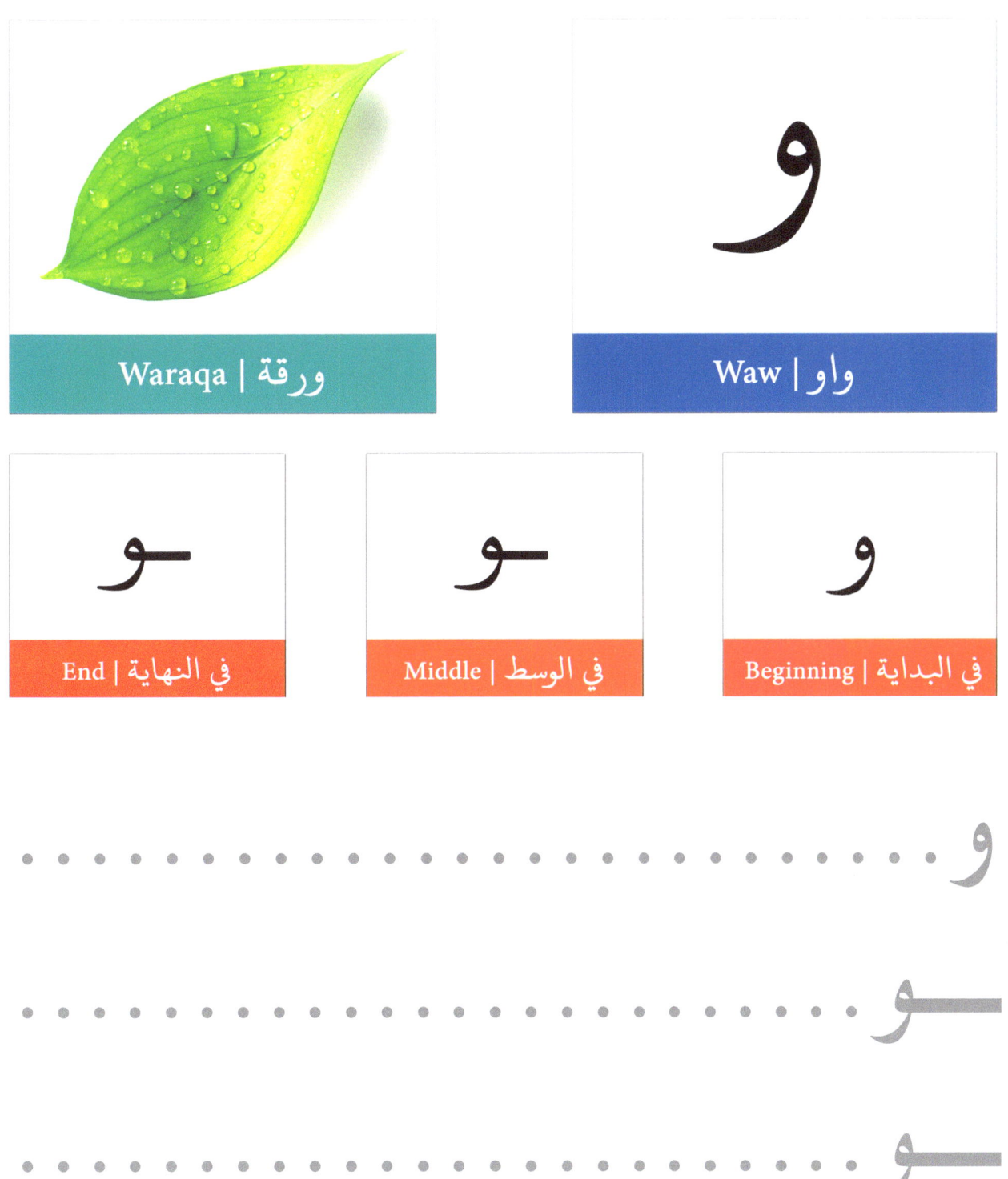

The Arabic Alphabet

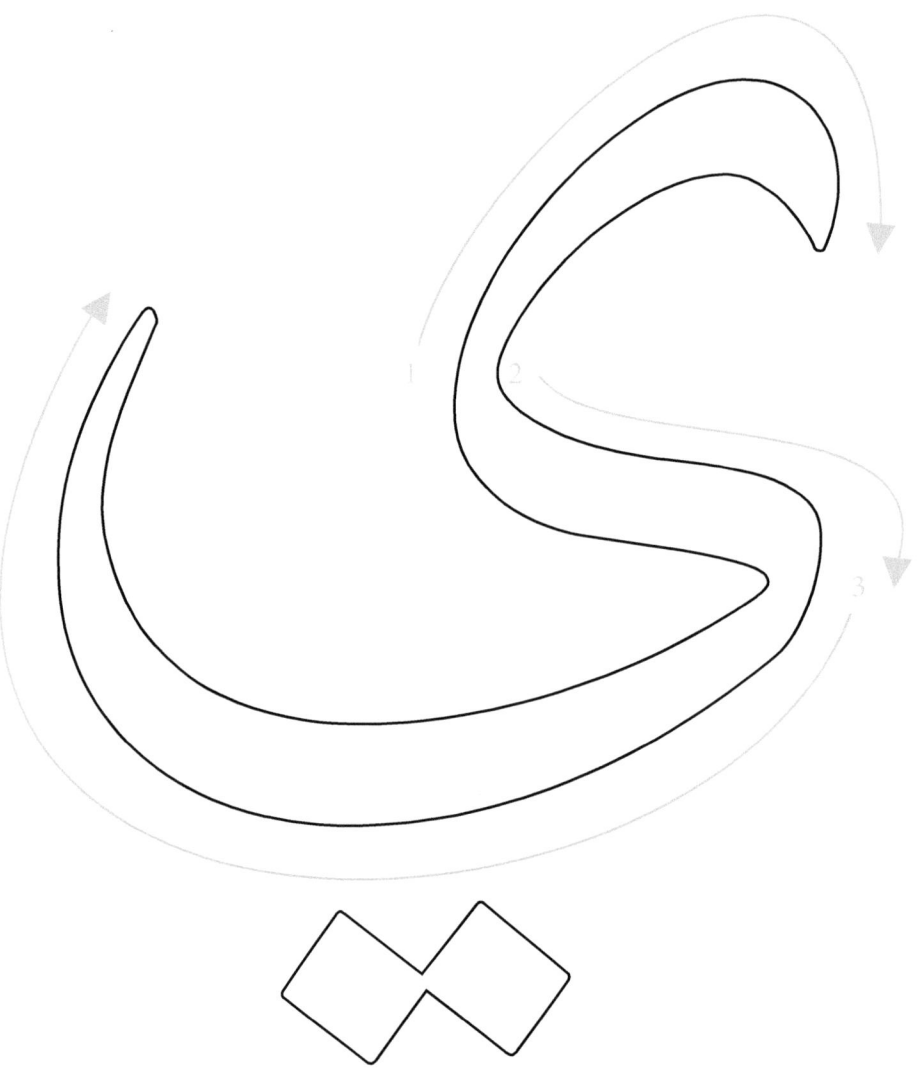

The Arabic Alphabet

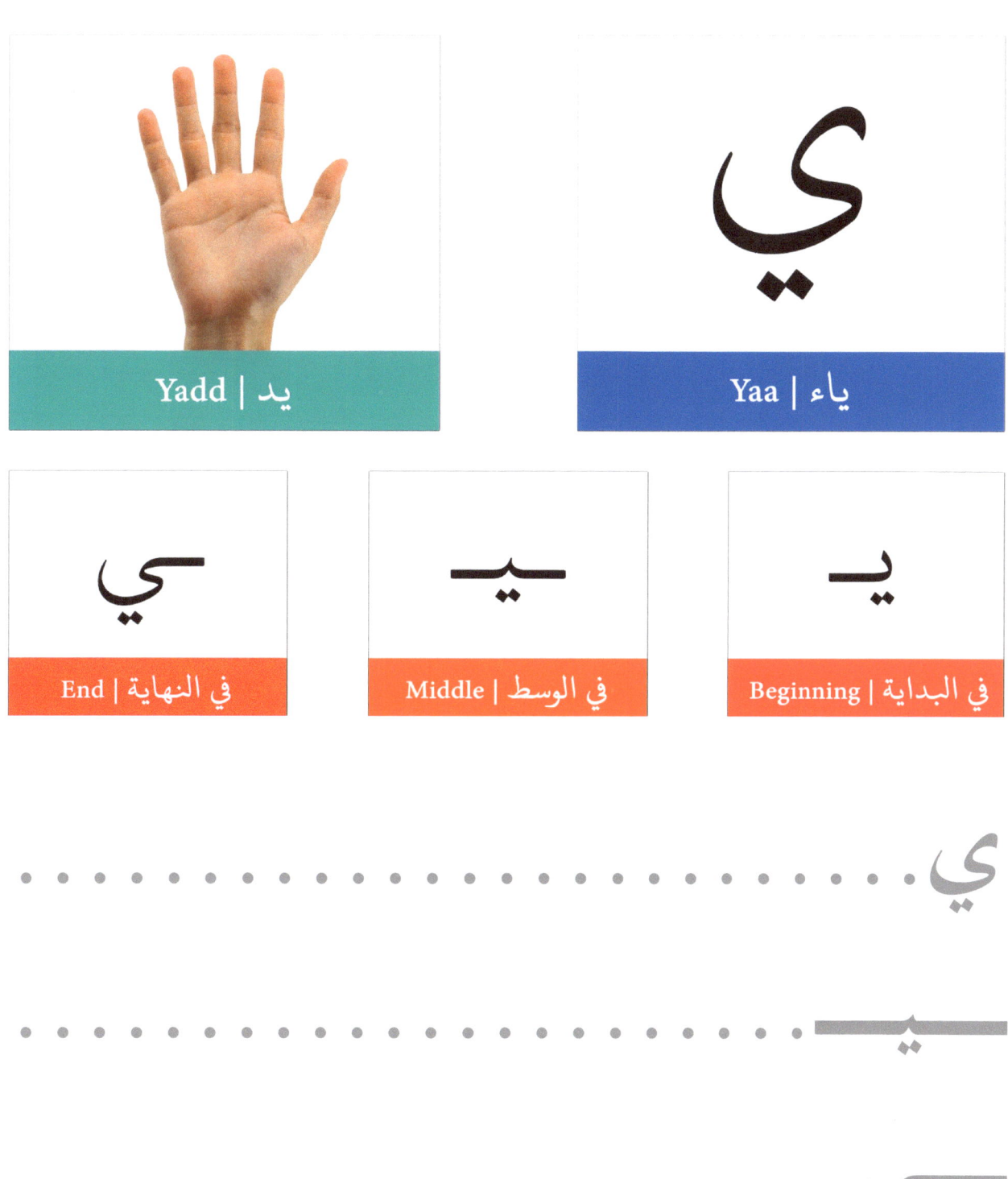

61

Also available by the same author...

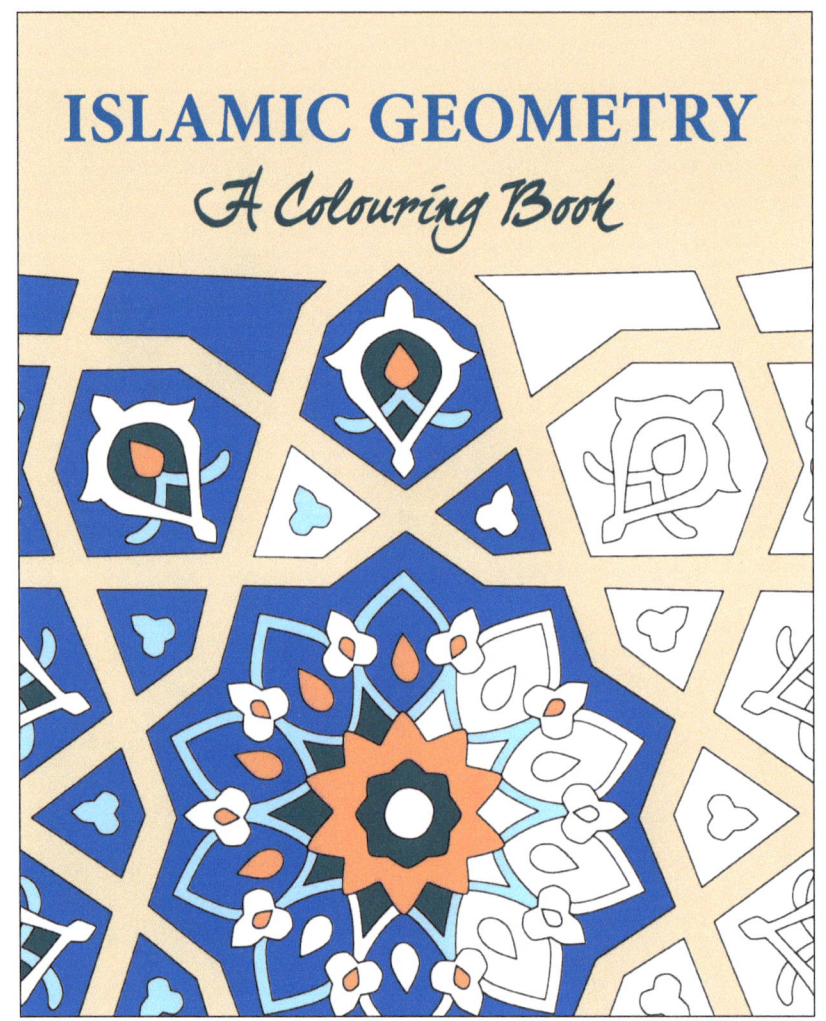

The Arabic Alphabet

The Arabic Alphabet

www.ingramcontent.com/pod-product-compliance
Lightning Source LLC
LaVergne TN
LVHW072126070426
835512LV00002B/17